HAL•LEONARD®
BANJO
PLAY-ALONG

AUDIO
ACCESS
INCLUDED

BLUEGRASS
★ Festival Favorites ★

Arranged and recorded by Mike Schmidt

Recording credits:
Mike Schmidt – Banjo, Guitar, Bass
Bruce King – Mandolin, Guitar

PLAYBACK+
Speed • Pitch • Balance • Loop

To access audio visit:
www.halleonard.com/mylibrary

Enter Code
8095-1751-9505-7564

ISBN 978-1-5400-2097-0

Visit Hal Leonard Online at
www.halleonard.com

Contact us:
Hal Leonard
7777 West Bluemound Road
Milwaukee, WI 53213
Email: info@halleonard.com

In Europe, contact:
Hal Leonard Europe Limited
42 Wigmore Street
Marylebone, London, W1U 2RN
Email: info@halleonardeurope.com

In Australia, contact:
Hal Leonard Australia Pty. Ltd.
4 Lentara Court
Cheltenham, Victoria, 3192 Australia
Email: info@halleonard.com.au

Performance Notes
By Mike Schmidt

Thank you for purchasing *Bluegrass Festival Favorites*. This is a collection of play-along tunes intended for the intermediate to advanced player of the five-string Bluegrass banjo. "Festival Favorites" refers to a collection of must-know tunes for the inevitable jam sessions that pop up at Bluegrass festivals, concerts, or wherever there are two or more like-minded musicians.

The tunes in this book are presented in several different keys. Because a capo is used, they're still written and played in a standard G tuning. So, for example, a tune in the key of A is capoed on the 2nd fret and still thought of, discussed, and played in terms of G. In this book, for the most part, the key of D is capoed on the 2nd fret and played in a C position. In this style of banjo playing, there are lots of open strings required, so with a capo, the banjo player can pretty much think in terms of the familiar keys of G and C. Of course, there are exceptions – one of the tunes in this book is in F! – but this covers a lot of the music we play and most of the tunes in this book. That said, remember that the Performance Notes section of this book makes references to G and C position, even though we might be in another key. Knowing the chord numbers is good, too. You know, the I, IV, and V symbols. Above the staves, the chords are shown two ways. For the banjo, the chords in parentheses show what you're playing, and the chords not in parentheses are the chords played by accompanists, in the true key. Bass, mandolin, and fiddle don't use capos, so this is for them.

Also, it's imperative to remember that, just because you see a given chord symbol written above the staff, it does not mean you, the banjo (or other solo instrument) player, should automatically put that chord position down on the neck. You're playing the melody and often play single notes through those chords. There are times when you will, particularly when you're playing backup chops, but it's not a given in lead parts. Please keep this in mind.

A significant part of learning any instrument is playing with others. This is important at any ability level. *Bluegrass Festival Favorites* and its accompanying audio are the answer. Each tune is presented twice: once with the full band so you can hear the banjo parts, and once without the banjo, so you can play along with the rest of the band. Because it's recorded, the band won't stop if you make a mistake. You will be trained to keep going no matter what happens, just like you would in a performance. Because the band doesn't stop, you need to pretend the mistake never happened and just keep going – a valuable skill!

You'll also want to consider the rhythm and speed at which the banjo is being played. This is an intermediate to advanced-level book, but the recorded tunes are still a bit slower than you might ultimately play them. Think of them as a learning tool, not backing tracks. With the reduced speed comes an occasional involuntary change to the rhythm of the notes. As written, you are looking at mostly eighth notes; as played, these all have equal value. This is true for medium and fast tempo tunes, but if you listen to a slower tune, you might notice the player tends to swing the note values slightly. By "swing," we mean that each pair of notes is played with a bit of a stagger. The first of the two is of slightly longer duration, while the second is slightly shorter. If you read music, you might think of it as if each pair of notes is a dotted eighth and a 16th note. It's easier to listen to the recording and feel it than to try to explain it in writing. Someone once said, "Talking about music is like dancing about architecture." I think that applies here. Compare the recordings of "Banks of the Ohio" and "Man of Constant Sorrow." That should explain it much better than I can here.

With the exception of "Banks of the Ohio" and "Eighth of January," which have three banjo breaks, every tune in this book has two. The first banjo break is a bit easier and the second is slightly more challenging. When playing along with the recording, remember you can substitute one break for any of the banjo parts on that recording. The chords are the same, so as soon as you know the first break, you can start practicing with the recording. The backup chords are provided for the other instrumental breaks, too.

Backup

As mentioned, we also address some basic backup techniques here. While not intended as a lesson book, this still warrants discussion. Since there are typically no percussion instruments in a Bluegrass band, other instruments can and do take these roles. It depends on the band, but often you'll find the banjo and mandolin appropriating the part of the snare drum when they're not taking a break, as you will hear in the play-along audio. During their lead breaks, both the banjo and mandolin are playing lots of rapid-fire notes, usually four notes to each beat. When one of these instruments is playing a solo, the other can play upbeats, not only to give that backbeat rhythm, but to get out of the soloist's way. Some banjo players choose to continue playing rolls behind a lead mandolin part; that can get cluttered and distract from the lead player. You will notice that, in these arrangements, when one instrument is playing a lead break, the other is playing the backbeat accompaniment. The other players will appreciate it if you choose to do upbeats rather than continuing to do rolls. You will see that, while I do write the backup parts here as upbeat chops, I occasionally throw in a tag lick at the end of a phrase; but still, it's minimal.

There are three positions for a major chord on the banjo: a barre chord, a D-position, and an F-position. This means you use the shape of a D or F chord, but on different frets to make different chords. A barre is simply putting one finger across all the strings on the same fret.

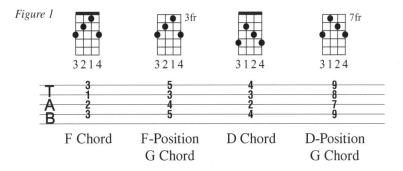

Figure 1

| F Chord | F-Position G Chord | D Chord | D-Position G Chord |

So, start by playing an F chord. If you move this up two frets, keeping the same finger position, it will become a G chord. A barre across the 5th fret is C, and on the 7th fret it's D.

The backup parts written in this book are not etched in stone; they are suggestions. As long as you play the right chords, you're free to do anything you like. For example, in some measures, the backup may alternate between two inversions (positions) of the same chord, but if you're more comfortable just staying on one of those positions, that's fine. If the book shows a bit of a tag lick at the end of a phrase and you'd rather play chops, go for it.

"Banks of the Ohio"

This is a Bluegrass standard, a great tune that embodies Bluegrass and Folk music: lost love, yearning, and murder. Our band learned it in the key of A because it was comfortable for the singers. For the banjo and probably guitar, that meant a capo on the 2nd fret and played in a G position. Later, playing with people who believed in doing things as close to original as possible, I needed to relearn my break in the key of F – not a common key for banjo, but not really that difficult with a bit of practice. Up to this tune, if we played in F, I usually capoed on the 5th fret and played in C position, but not here. This one's for real. But never fear: We have two more breaks in G-position, so you can use whatever you like; and with this tune, the key change doesn't require repositioning the capo.

The first challenge shows up in measures 5 and 6. Because you're playing the lead here, you need to play a B♭ note, making your left-hand position a C7; basically, a C, but you add the pinky to the 3rd fret of the 3rd string. Down close to the nut, it can be a bit of a stretch, but if you haven't been using this particular C7, I think you'll find it useful up the neck, as well.

Watch for the B♭ chord. Technically, this can be done with a simple barre across the 3rd fret, but there's a hammer-on in measure 12, so hold a barre chord for measure 11, and then on measure 12, hold the barre through beat 1, then lift and play the notes individually. Measure 14 is similar. Measure 13 is a full F chord and measure 14 is freehand again.

The mandolin break is in F as well, so we'll have a bit of practice doing backup in the key of F, but the last thing the mandolin (and other accompaniment) does is hit a D. This is called a pivot chord, making for a comfortable key change into G. Following that are the aforementioned banjo breaks in the key of G.

A few things to watch for are the eighth-note hammer-ons in measures 12, 14, 15, 37, 41, and 62. These are played the same speed as normal picked notes. Finally, beat 4 of measure 14 is a triplet, consisting of a pick, a hammer-on, and a pull-off, all in the space of a single beat. Space them evenly on beat 4. Listening to the recording is probably easier to understand than reading about it here.

"Cotton Eyed Joe"

Like "Cumberland Gap," "Cotton Eyed Joe" is a tune of near infinite variations. It took quite a bit of research to land on an arrangement that would reflect all of them and still sound like the standard it is. This one has a few interesting oddities.

For one thing, there are some half measures, or one-beat measures. Speaking in terms of the capoed banjo, the final D chord of each verse is one beat, and it's an extra beat, so it gets its own measure. This happens on measure 20 in the first banjo break, measure 42 in the mandolin break, and again on measure 64 in the second banjo break.

Notice that a measure is added to each break. The very end of the "B" part of every break includes an extra, one-measure tag lick. This is common in old-timey tunes, and "Cotton Eyed Joe" definitely is that. You'll find these right after the one-beat measures described above, at measures 21, 43, and 65.

Between measures 51 and 52, there's an interesting little thing: a pull-off across a barline. Like some of the others, it's best to listen to it a few times, slowed down. Figure 2 is basically the same lick without the pull-off, so if you have any trouble with it, try this first; once you're comfortable with it, sneak in the pull-off.

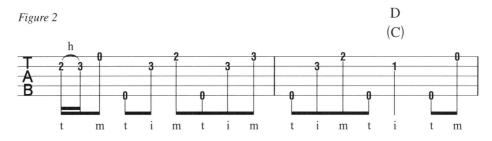

Figure 2

Finally, there's a bend in measure 56. This is a half-step bend, meaning the pitch goes up the equivalent of one fret. Figure 3 shows how it might sound, and could also be an alternate for this measure if you prefer. The open 2nd string would replace the bend.

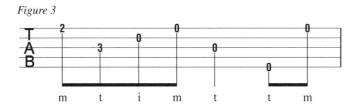

Figure 3

Fret the 1st string 2nd fret with the index finger and the 3rd string 3rd fret with the middle, regardless of which version of this measure you play.

"Cumberland Gap"

Here's another Bluegrass standard, and there are as many variations on how to play it as there are recordings. I found multiple recordings by a given player, who played it differently from one to the other. Like most music in this style there are two parts, commonly referred to as verse and chorus. Sometimes we call the verse the "A" part and the chorus the "B" part. Of course, these have nothing to do with the key. A is part one, and B is part two. The arrangement here is in an A-A-B-A form. Measures 1-8 is the first A part; 9-16 make up the second A; 17-24 are B; and 25-32 are back to the final A. Don't confuse these form letters with the boxed section letters that run alphabetically throughout each tune.

In the B part (measures 17-24 in the first break and 81-88 in the second break), you're basically holding an Am position (see Figure 4) on the 8th and 9th frets, and the movement on the 10th and 11th frets is taken care of with the pinky.

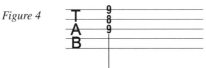

Figure 4

While the melody may seem repetitive, it's a great tune for you to show off – normally played at least half again as fast as it appears on the recording.

We'll explore endings in the pages ahead, but here's an example of one of the mix-and-match endings. Measures 97 and 98 are Ending 3A; 99 and 100 are Ending 2B. Notice also that the last two notes are written on both the 1st and 5th strings. Choose either, not both.

"Eighth of January"

This is one of two tunes in this book presented in two keys. Being a fiddle melody, the keys of A and D are both common. Because we're using a capo, they're both in G position for us; it's just the capo that's changed. Not many banjo players capo on the 7th fret for the key of D, but it's a great sound. Don't overuse it, but for numbers like this, "Soldier's Joy," and "Liberty," it sounds really fine.

The first banjo break is in A. At the end of that break, it immediately changes to the key of D at measure 17, where the banjo begins backup for the mandolin (still capoed on the 2nd fret).

The second banjo break begins with the pickups to measure 33, capoed on the 7th fret. Here, we can pause the recording, change the capo, tune it up, etc. In real life, it might not be that easy, so keep in mind this is mainly for demonstration of the two keys. If you play it with a band, odds are you'll either play it through in one key, or you'll go back and forth between instruments; having to change your capo is unlikely. Measures 29-32 are written as rests, except for the pickups to measure 33, which start the banjo break in D.

Notice also the second banjo break goes through twice, so you have three breaks total.

"Liberty"

Unlike the others, this one starts with a mandolin break. In fact, there's a little two-measure pickup. This is a fiddle tune, so the mandolin is taking the fiddle's place. This way, when the first break is done, there's a nice transition into the banjo part. Notice that, in the chorus ("B" part), the chord progression differs slightly between the banjo and mandolin parts. The mandolin plays it as a fiddler would (the way most people do), in the usual progression. But the banjo part is a variation Doug Dillard used to do, so this chorus is slightly different. In measures 52 and 102, there's a one-beat IV chord. (We're playing in a G-position, so it's a quick C chord.)

Without getting too detailed… If you're playing at this level, you're most likely improvising already, and it's fine to do that here, as well. Look at measure 38, for example. The penultimate note of the measure is an open 1st string. Sometimes, I'll keep the 1st string fretted on the 5th fret. Try it both ways and see what you prefer.

"Man of Constant Sorrow"

As with other songs in this book, be aware of the difference between eighth-note hammer-ons and 16th-note hammer-ons. Compare those in measures 1 and 11 to the one in measure 17.

Notice measure 34. In terms of G-position, you've been playing a G for the past five measures; except for here, the last measure before the C. Often, before a C, you might play a G7... well, here, we're playing a VII chord... an F! Instead of just a G chord with an F note added, we're playing the whole F chord. It's a cool effect if you don't overdo it.

Three measures later (37–38), we have a D chord, but notice the thumb note goes between 11 and 12. The 12th fret makes it a Dsus4 chord, another ornamental touch I like to do. This is similar to the 1st string 3rd fret move in measure 16. Start with a regular C chord in measure 15, then bring the 1st string up a fret, and back down.

Measure 45 is interesting in that it uses a bit of a Reno-style lick, meaning you play the same string more than once while alternating fingers on the right hand. In the second half of that measure, you play the 4th string open, then the 2nd fret, then the 3rd string open and 2nd fret. Each pair of notes is picked with index, then thumb. If it's more comfortable, you could reverse the right-hand fingers and do thumb, then index. Try both and see what you prefer. In measure 47, we have a similar pattern. Be aware of the last two notes of that measure, where you use the thumb twice in a row, breaking one of the early rules: "Never pick with the same finger twice in a row, unless there's a rest between them." Rules are made to be broken.

"Roll in My Sweet Baby's Arms"

We start off with exceptions to the rules. First, because there's an eight-beat solo introduction by the banjo, we have only a four-beat countoff. On the first listen, it's not a big deal, but when you start playing with the recording (and no banjo), you will need to keep this in mind. Enter on the fourth click.

Most instrumental breaks are either the verse or the chorus of the song. For this one, it's both. I've heard several recordings where two instruments split a verse/chorus break. While we didn't do that in this recording, we did give you two verses and two choruses to arrange any way you like.

This tune is straightforward, with no big surprises or tricky bits. You might notice at measures 63 and 64, however, that you switch the back rhythm to downbeats rather than the upbeats you've been doing. They also move in a descending pattern of G, F, Em, Dm, following the bass line. (Remember we're capoed, playing in A but thinking in terms of G.) Measure 63 uses the D-position chords and 64 continues down the neck, changing to the Dm position. It's a way of bringing out, or anticipating, the G7 feel, preparing for the C chord in measure 65. Another way of saying this is I, VII, vi, v, leading to the IV.

"Wildwood Flower"

In "Wildwood Flower," pay attention to the type of hammer-ons we're using. Throughout the first break, there are no typical hammer-ons consisting of two 16th notes and an eighth note. Instead, they are all eighth-note hammers, so they're played at the same speed as the regular picked notes, a bit slower than the usual hammer-on. You can hear these in the recording.

In the backup, at measure 22, notice the first chord is a Dsus4, fretting the 8th fret of the 2nd string. This is optional, and if you prefer to barre your index finger across the 7th fret for both, go right ahead. Later in the backup, at measures 30 and 31, we do the same little run we described in "Roll in My Sweet Baby's Arms" at measures 63 and 64. Remember, use these kinds of things sparingly. Too much of anything gets monotonous for both you and the listener.

The second banjo break throws in a few melodic runs, but nothing too complicated. The first beat of measure 49 is a D-position G chord, but it's not played all on the beat. It is a bit of an arpeggio, meaning a chord played one note at a time. We do it with thumb, index, and middle, in that order. The thumb and index are just a tad in front of the beat, with the middle finger picking the 1st string on the beat. Listen to the recording.

Endings

We've included a bonus section here. This is a mix-and-match set of standard Bluegrass endings. By mix-and-match, we mean lots of classic endings have a start and a finish, a first and a second half, an A and a B. These, incidentally, are often referred to as "shave and a haircut" endings, for just that reason. The first half (the A part) sets it up and the second half (the B part) drives it home.

In many cases, the B section aligns with the syllables, "shave and a haircut, two bits." Ending 1 is one of the best-known of these, and is exactly that. You can sing the words with the B part. (If only a shave and a haircut were two bits today, huh?) Extra credit for knowing how much two bits is.

Basically, if you play across the pages, the A part and the B part match up pretty well; however, you can take any A part and match it up with any B part. Some work better than others, but it's up to you. Often, the contrasts between one ending and another are slight. In lines 1 and 2, there are few differences between the A and B parts. These would be good candidates for switches: 1A with 2B, or vise versa.

Notice also, on the B parts for 1, 2, and 3, the last two notes ("two bits") are played either on the 1st string or the 5th. I tend to use the 5th since they're the same notes, so it's your choice. Either one is correct. If you're more comfortable on one or the other, go for it; they're interchangeable.

Ending 6 is nice straight across, but 6A and 2B (or 5B) is a good combination, too. And these are only a few. There are lots more. See if you can invent more. Basically, just have fun with them!

Ending 1

The A part is rather straightforward. In the B part, however, there are a few tricks. Immediately, you're bending the second string on the first beat. You don't have to, but as written and played here, it's being done. Also, on the last beat of that same measure, you pick a 3rd string, 7th fret, but upon picking it, you slide upward. A more basic version, without the bends and slides, might be shown here in Figures 5 and 6. Notice the final two notes ("two bits") are played on the first string.

Figure 5   *Figure 6*

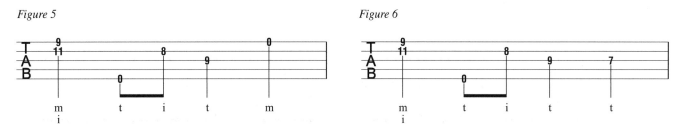

Ending 2

Similar to Ending 1, this has a few variations in the A part. Then, in the B part, what was a quarter note "pinch" on the first beat (the 11–9 combination) is now the same notes, but played sequentially as eighth notes. The 7 at the end of the first measure of part B can be played as is, or, as shown in Figures 5 and 6 above.

The final two notes here are played on the 5th string. The pitches are identical, so find the one that works best for you, and use it.

Ending 3

Still reminiscent of Endings 1 and 2, this Ending starts to change a bit in the timing and notes. In the first measure of part B, the 10–9 combination could be 11–9. Try it. And the last note of that same measure could be 1st string open or 3rd string 7th fret (with or without the slide. And in the final measure, 16 and 17, again, on 1st or 5th string.

Figure 7   *Figure 8*

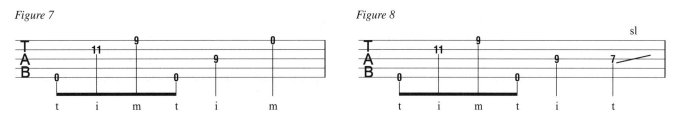

Ending 4

We're starting to stray further from the original. Still interchangeable with the others, but with some variations.

Ending 5

Part A of this one is a bit closer to the first few, but Part B is a nice, solid, syncopated ending.

Ending 6

This one is a good ending for a banjo-fiddle duet. Often, in a traditional fiddle tune, the banjo and fiddle play Part A together, note-for-note, then split away from each other for Part B. For an effective variation, play 6A then 2B.

So, between mixing and matching, and trying the variations shown here in the Performance Notes, you should have a good start on several ear-catching "Shave and a Haircut" endings.

Banks of the Ohio

19th Century Western American

G tuning:
(5th-1st) G-D-G-B-D

Keys of F and G

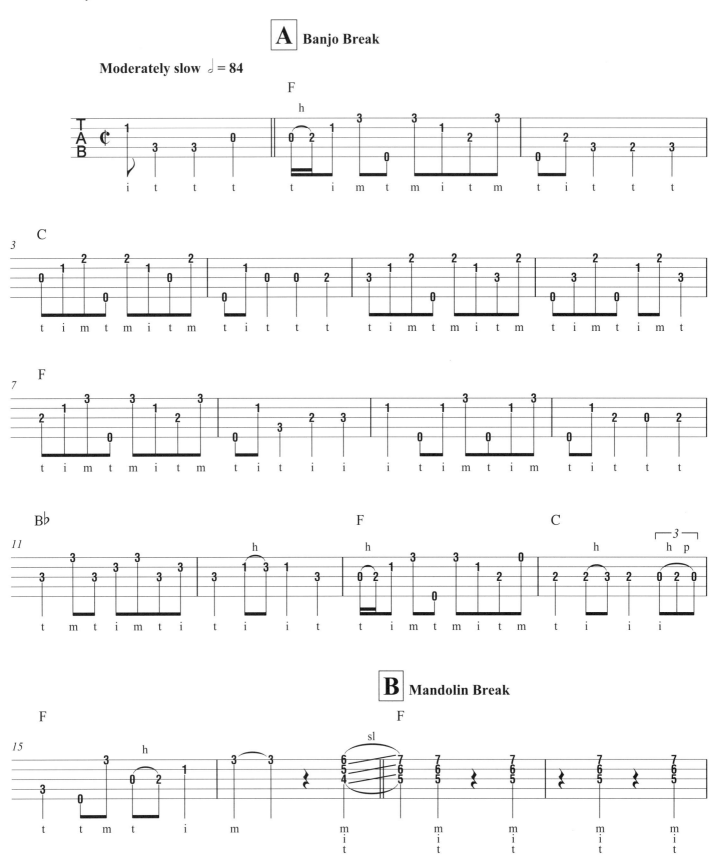

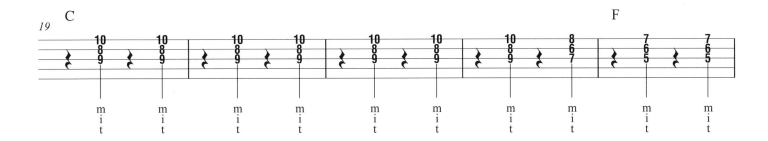

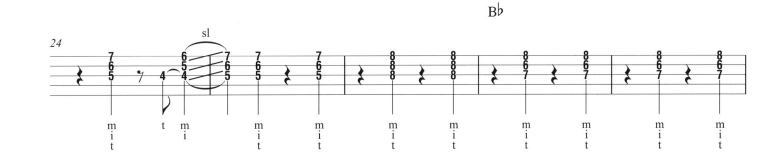

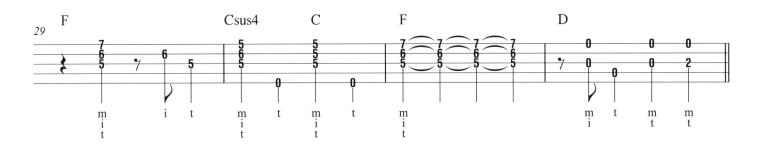

C Banjo Break

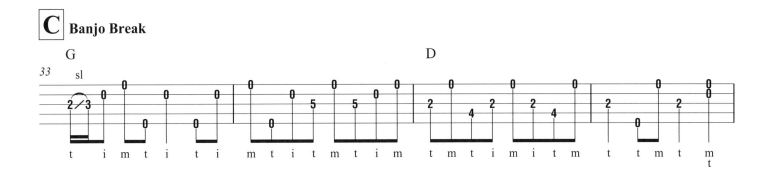

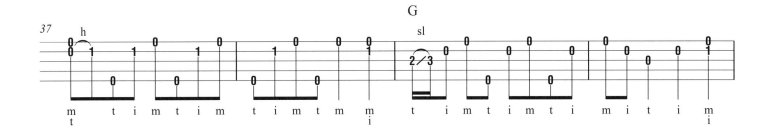

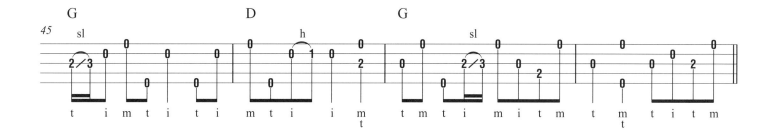

D Banjo Break

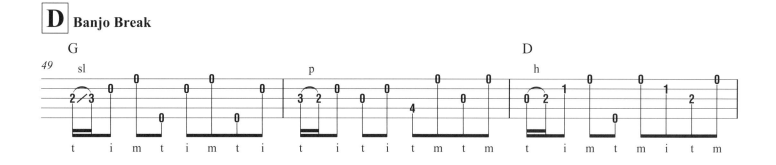

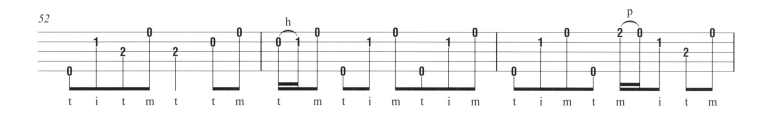

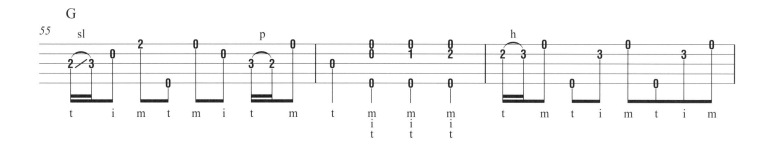

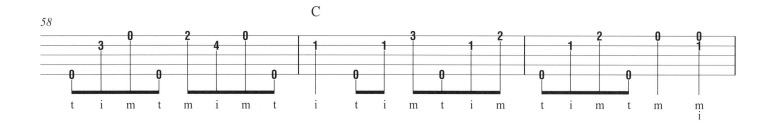

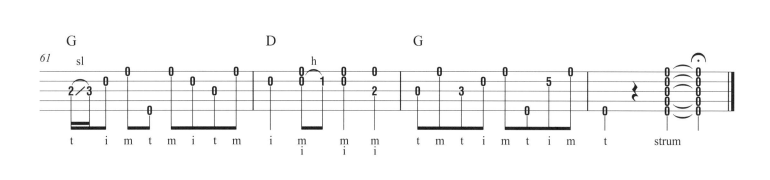

Cumberland Gap

Traditional

G tuning:
(5th-1st) G-D-G-B-D

Key of G

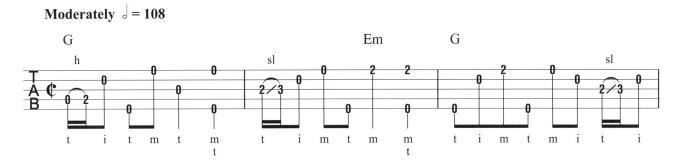

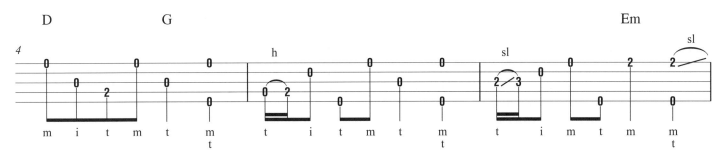

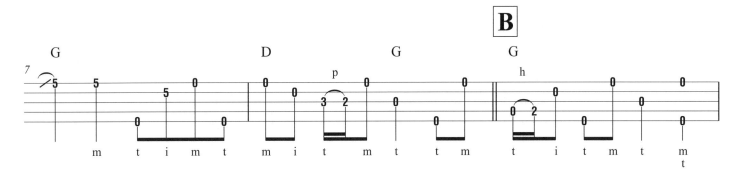

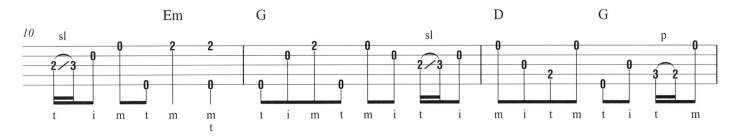

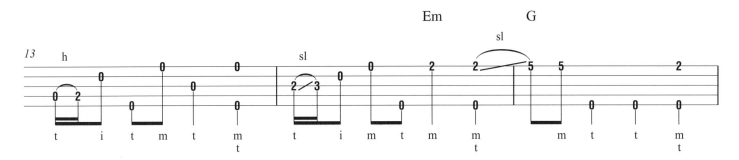

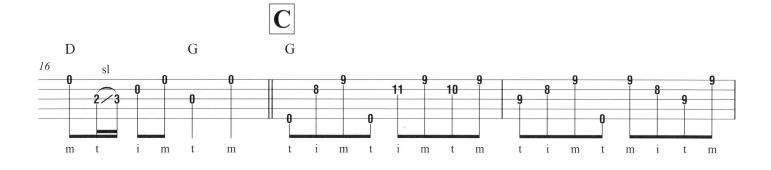

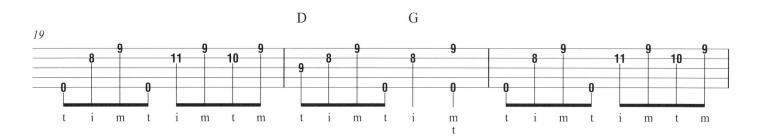

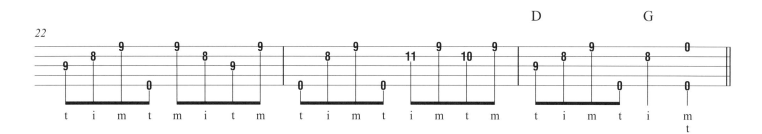

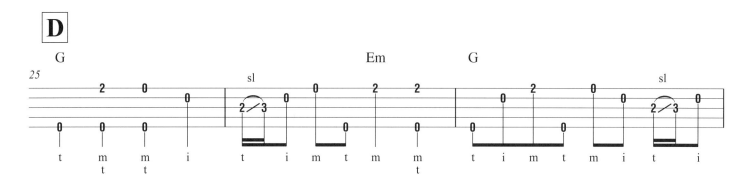

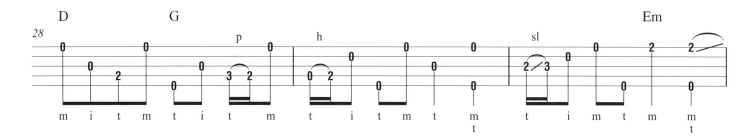

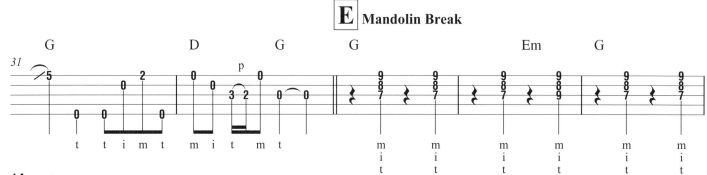

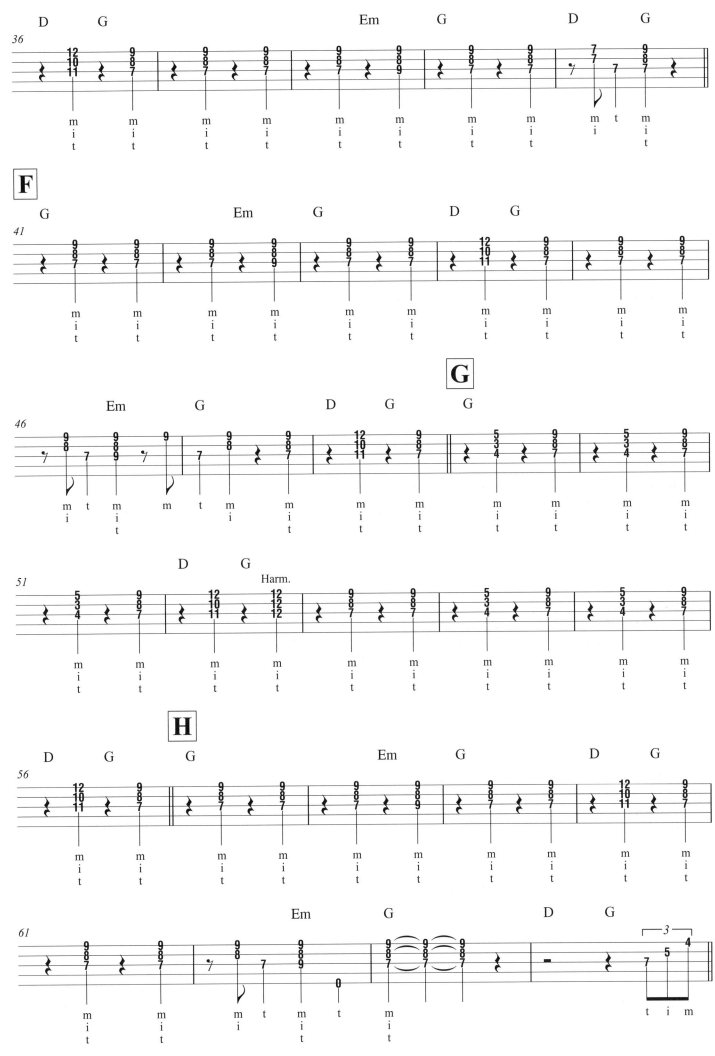

I Banjo Break

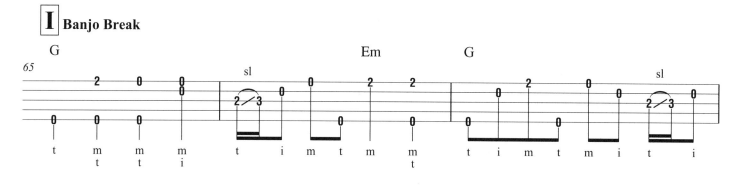

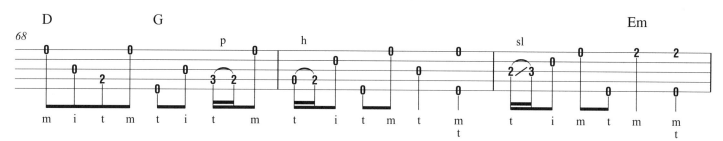

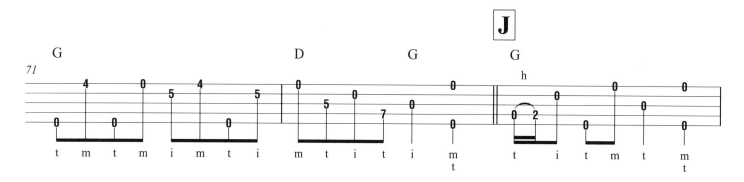

J

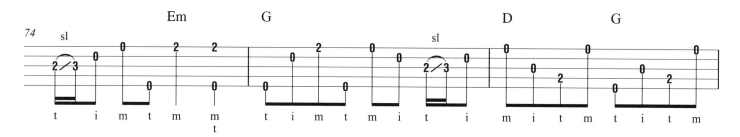

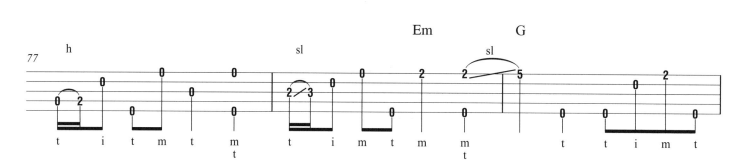

K

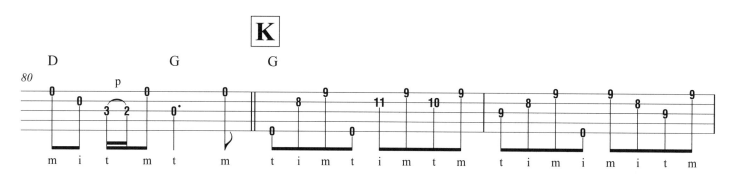

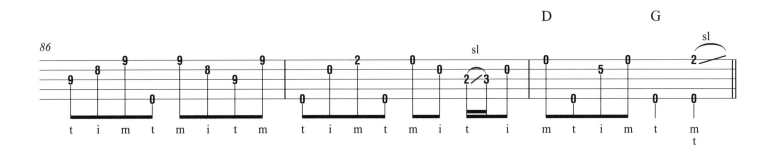

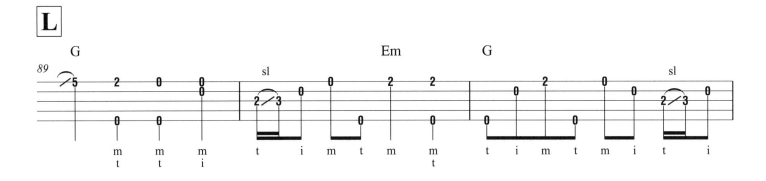

L

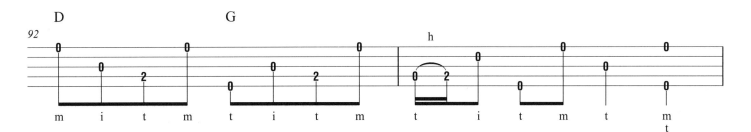

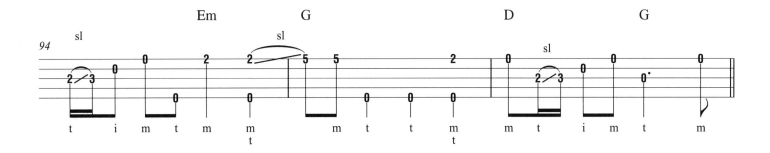

M Ending

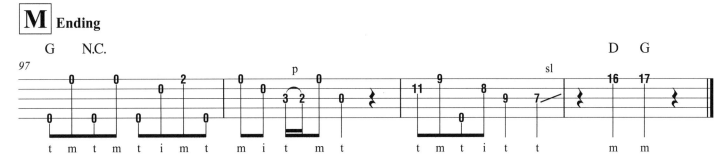

Cotton Eyed Joe

Tennessee Folksong

G tuning:
(5th-1st) G-D-G-B-D

Key of A
Capo II

A **Banjo Break**

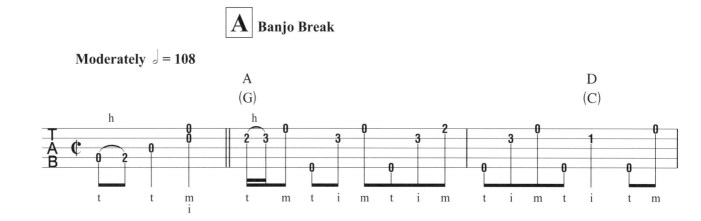

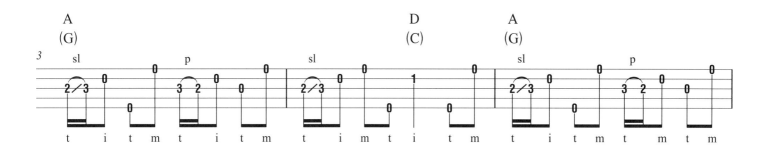

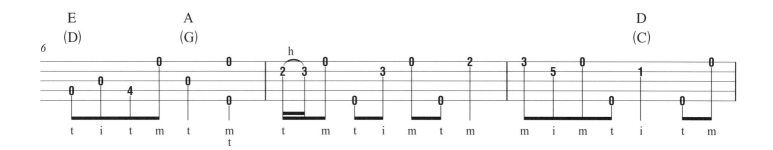

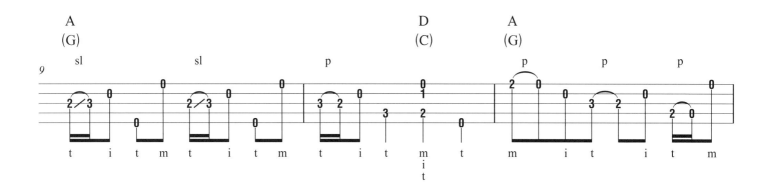

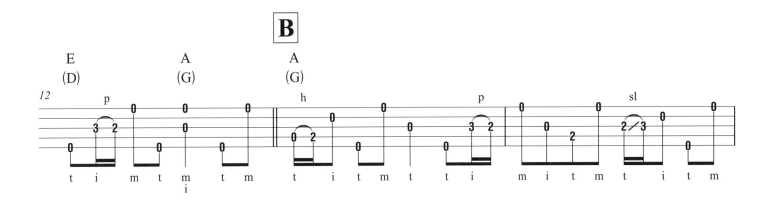

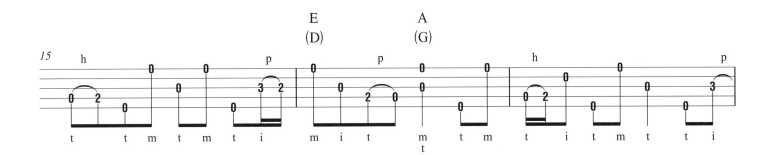

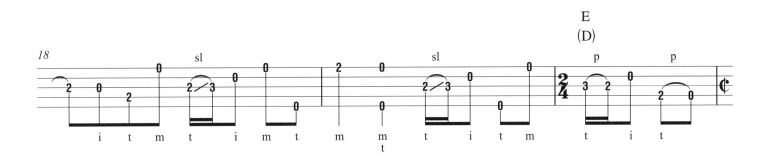

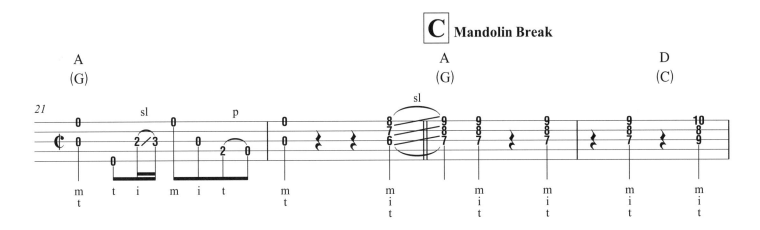

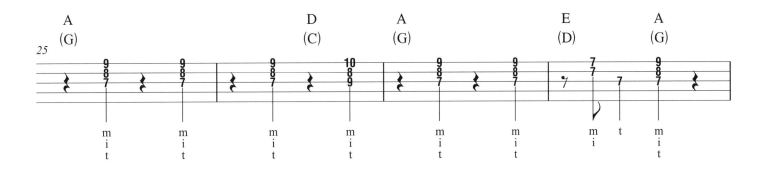

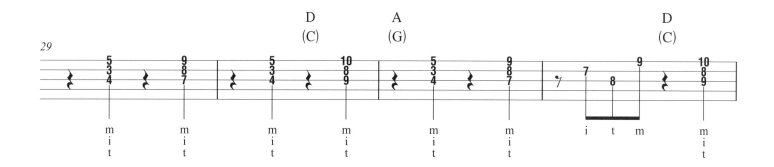

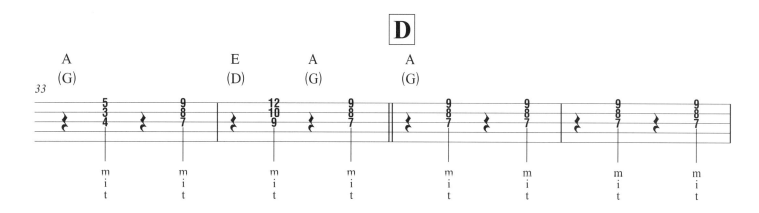

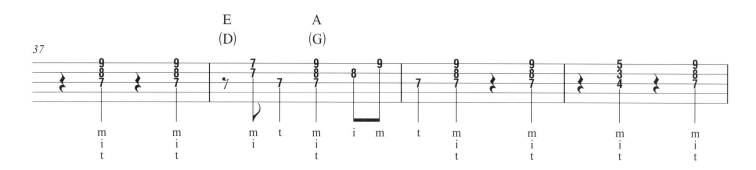

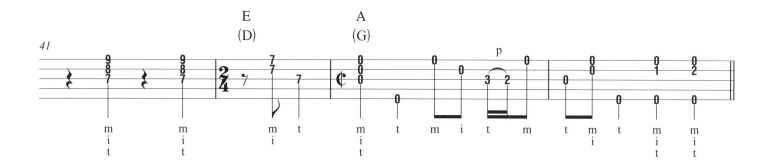

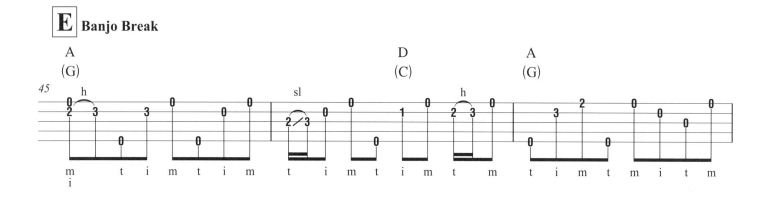

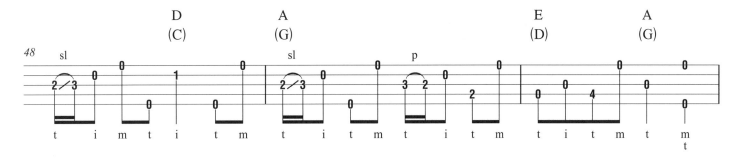

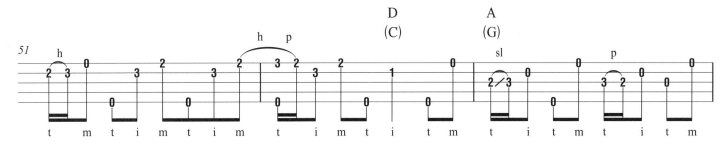

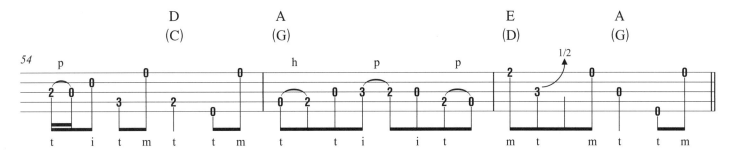

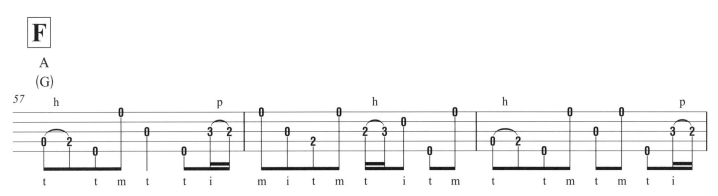

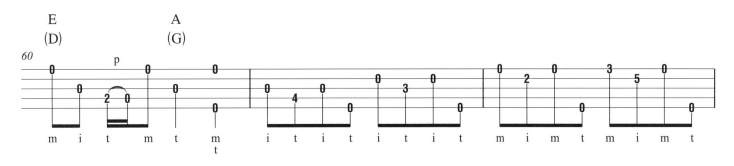

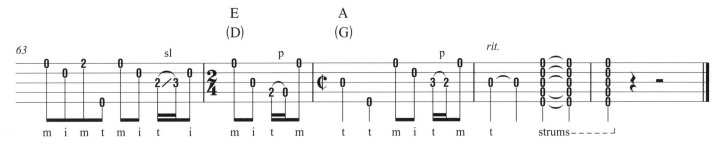

Eighth of January

Traditional

G tuning:
(5th-1st) G-D-G-B-D

Key of A
Capo II

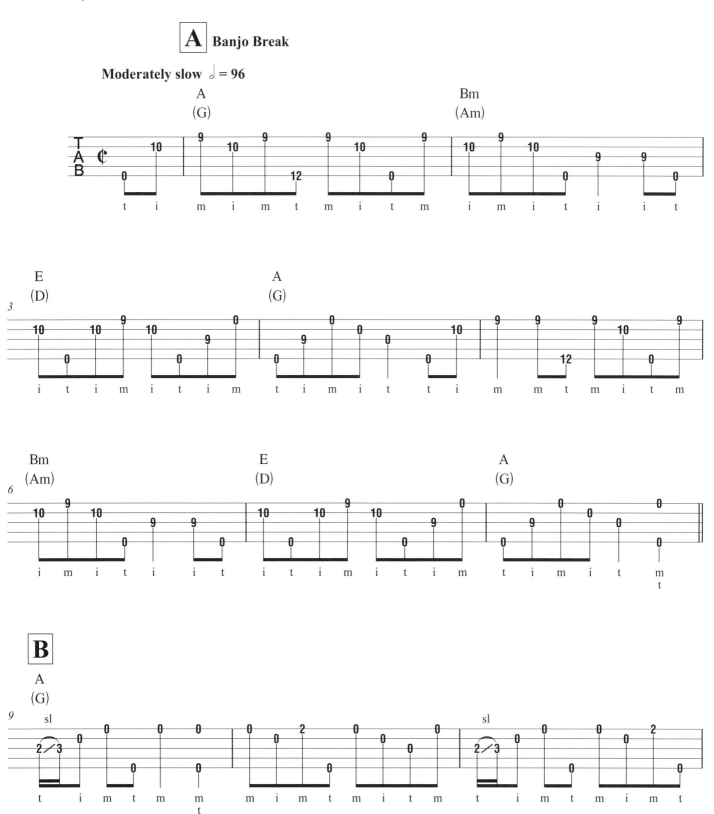

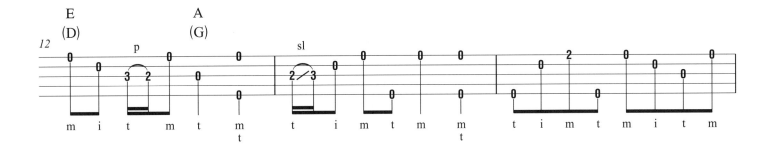

Key of D

C Mandolin Break

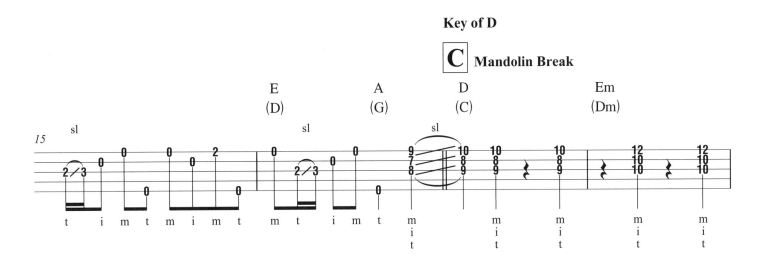

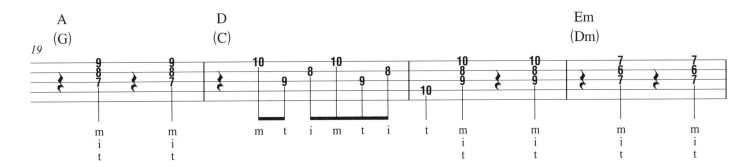

D

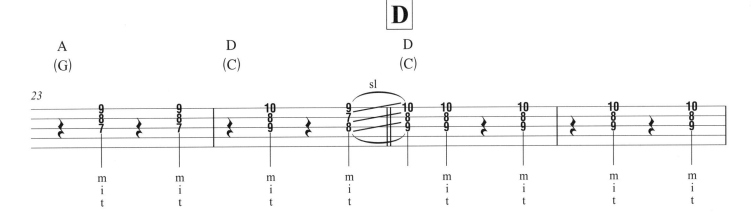

*Capo VII

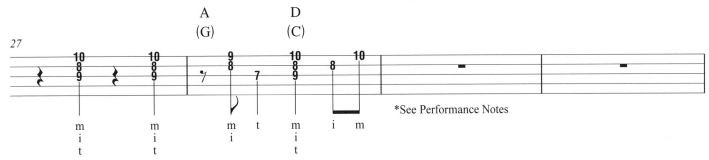

*See Performance Notes

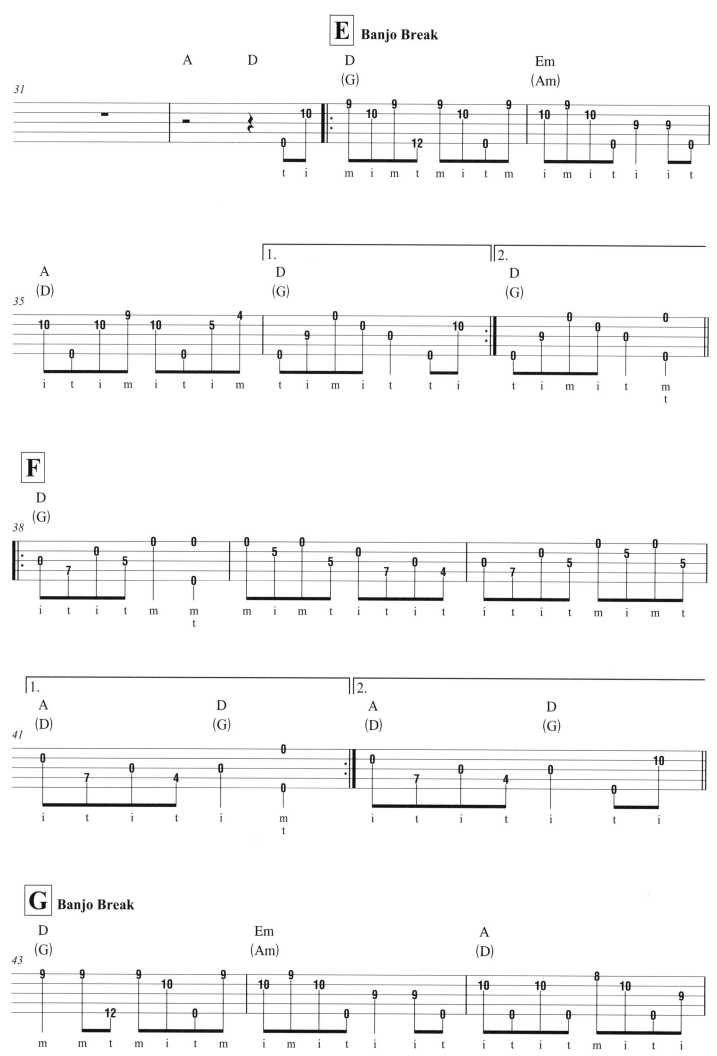

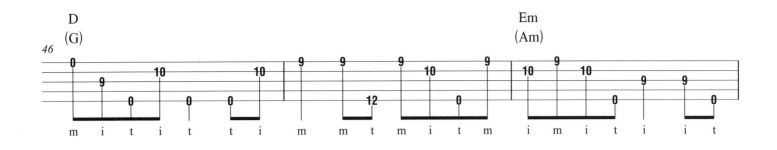

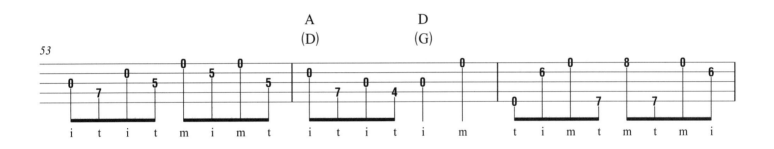

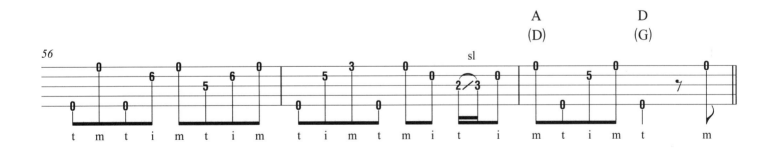

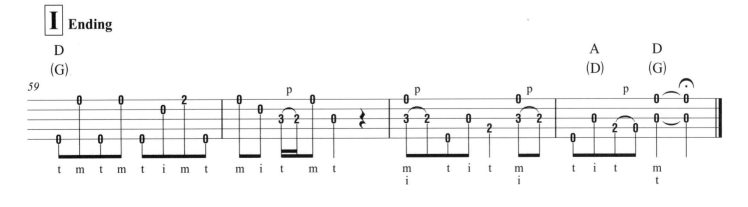

Liberty

Traditional

G tuning:
(5th-1st) G-D-G-B-D

Key of D
Capo VII

 **Mandolin Break**

Moderately slow ♩ = 92

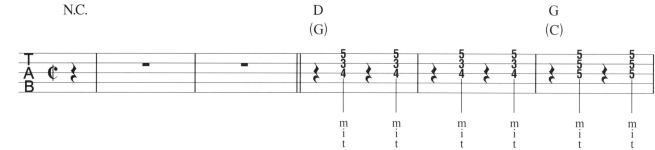

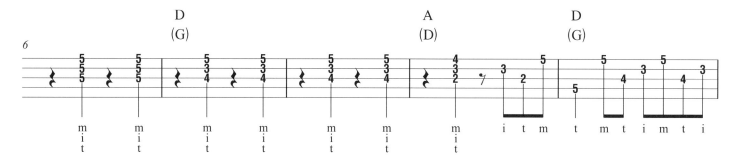

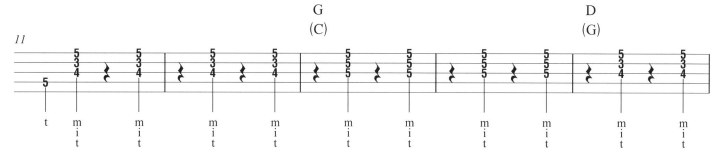

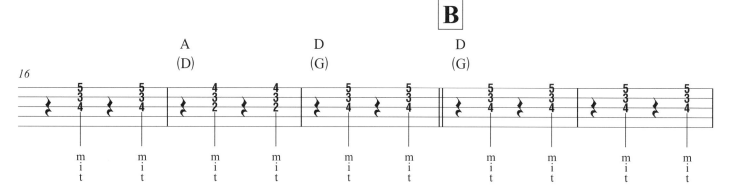

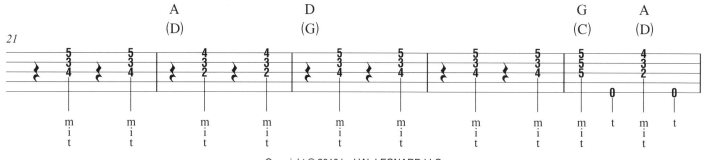

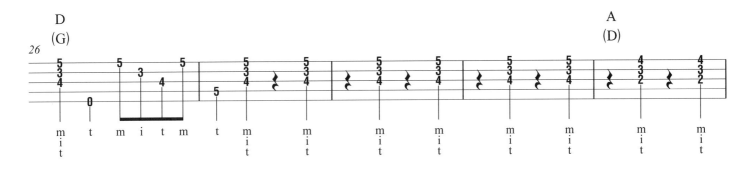

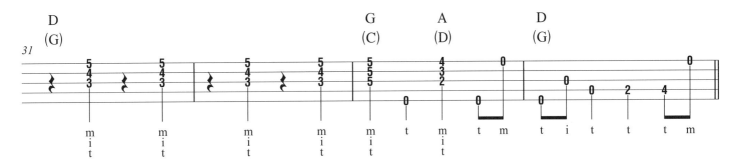

C Banjo Break

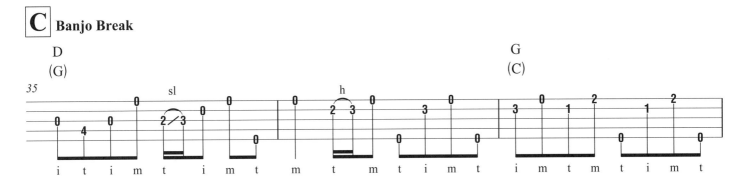

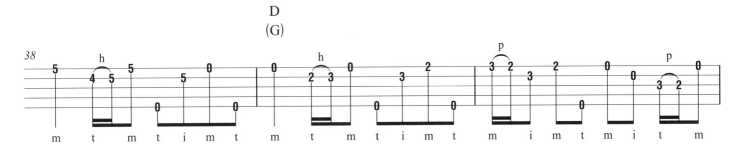

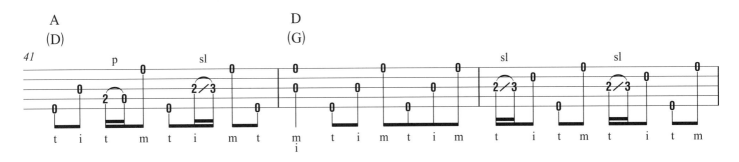

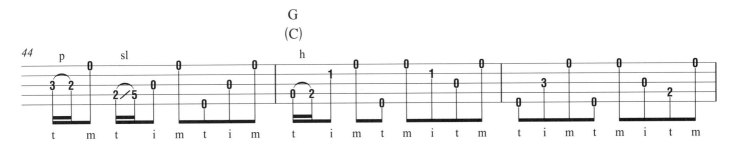

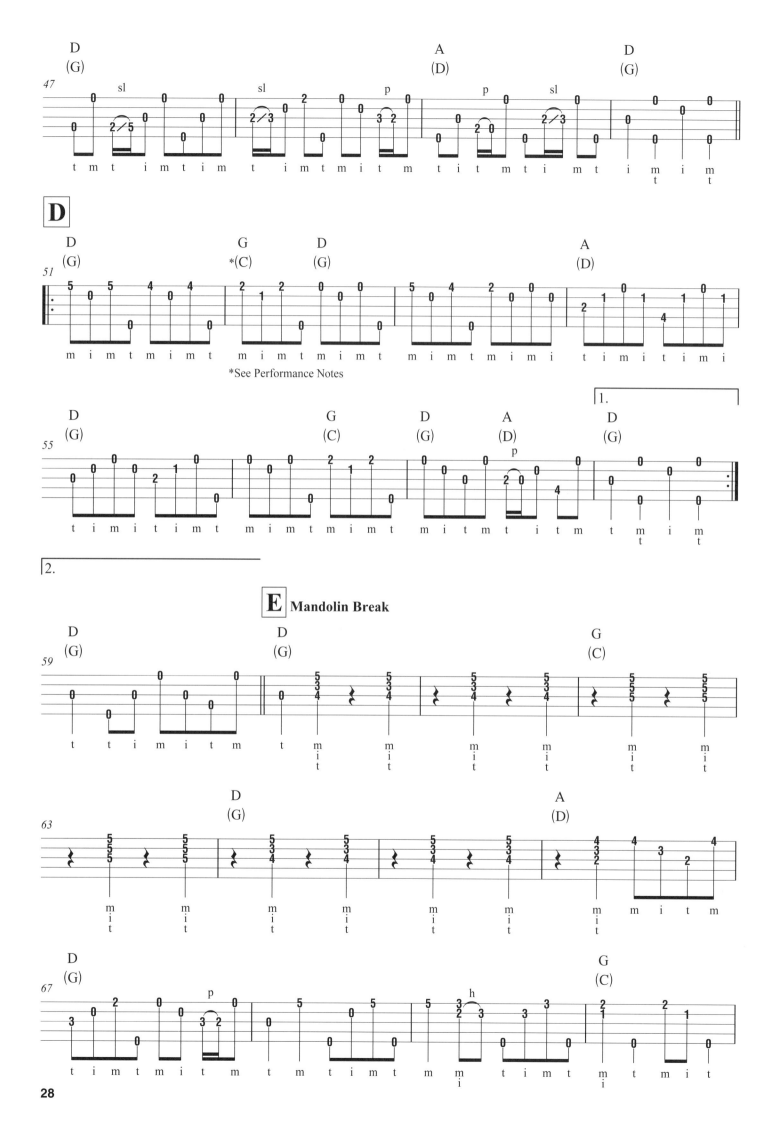

*See Performance Notes

E Mandolin Break

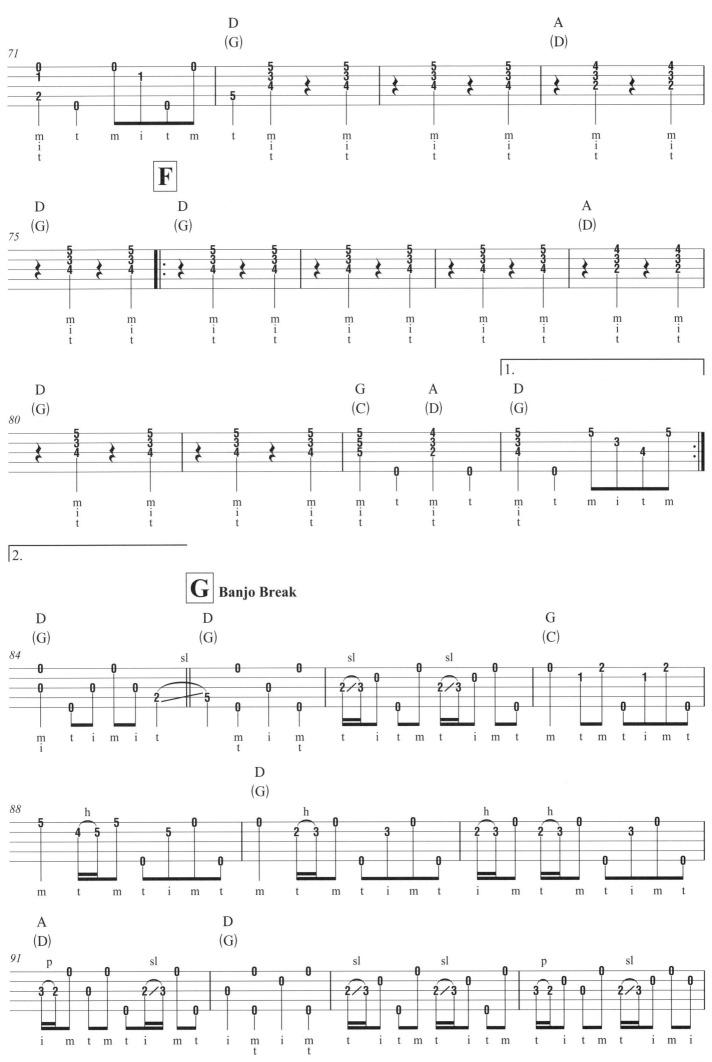

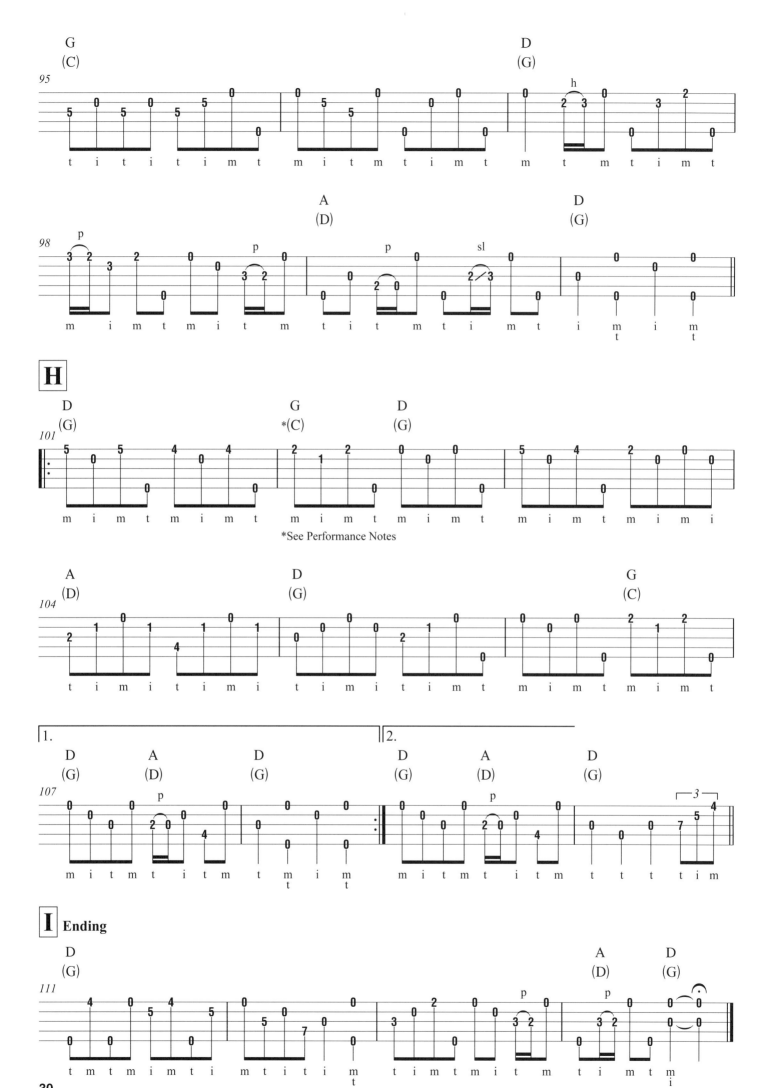

*See Performance Notes

H

I Ending

Man of Constant Sorrow

Traditional

G tuning:
(5th-1st) G-D-G-B-D

Key of A
Capo II

 **Banjo Break**

Moderately slow ♩ = 92

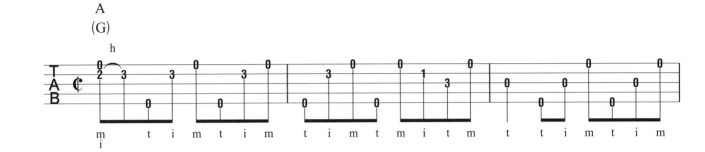

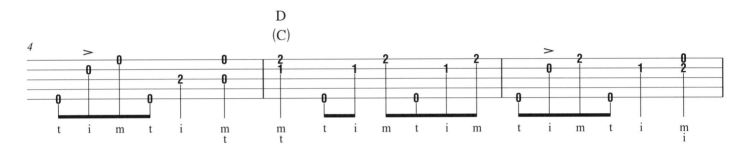

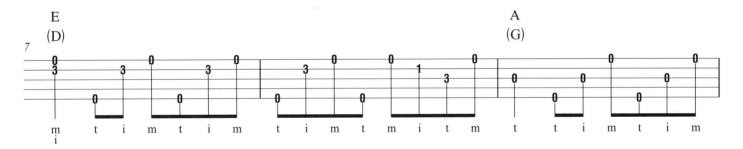

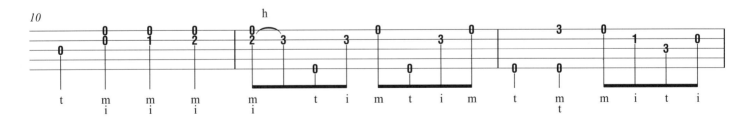

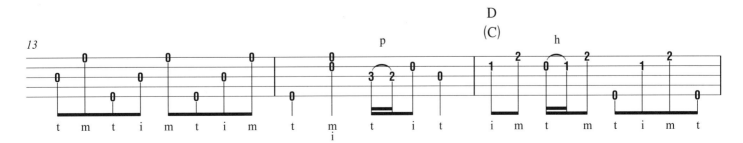

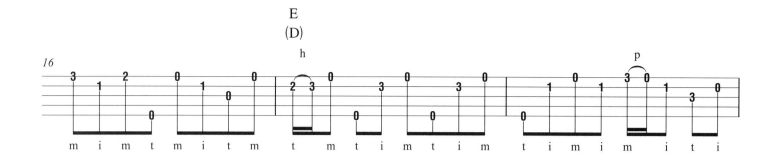

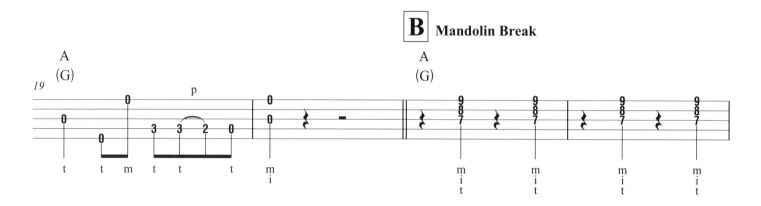

B Mandolin Break

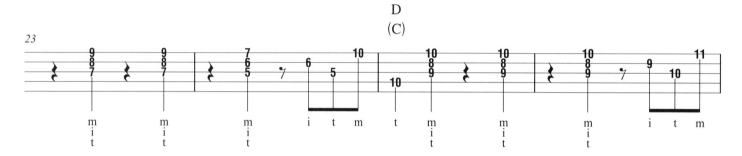

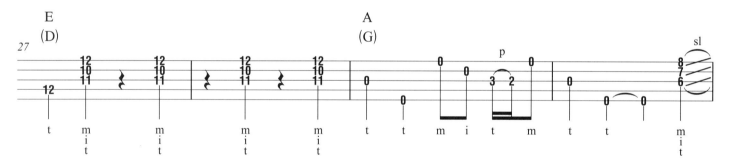

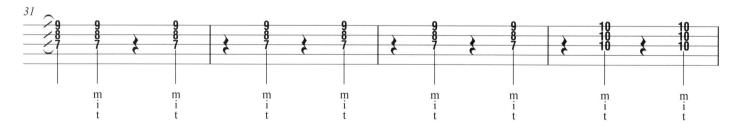

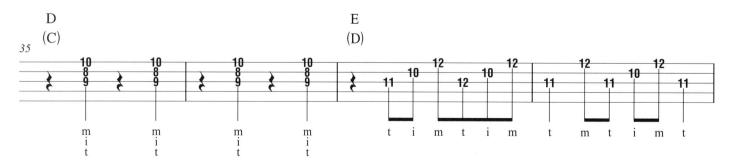

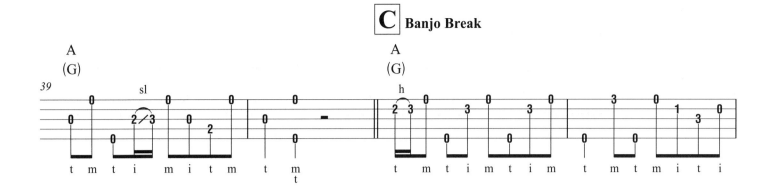

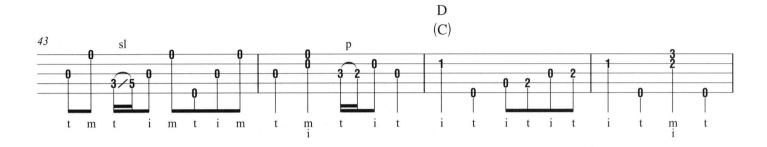

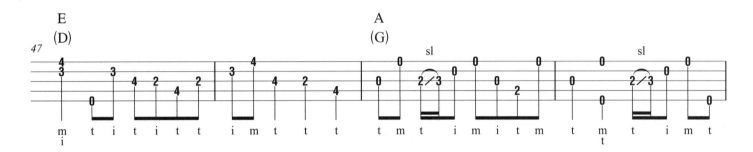

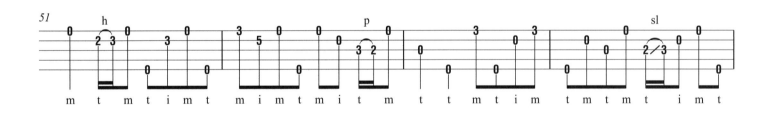

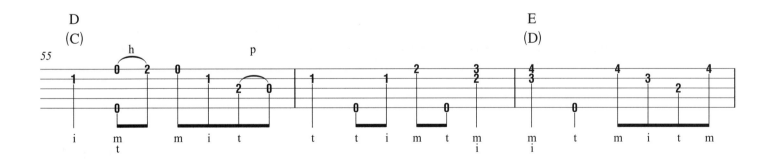

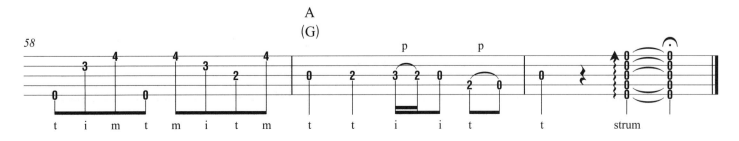

Roll in My Sweet Baby's Arms

Traditional

G tuning:
(5th-1st) G-D-G-B-D

Key of A
Capo II

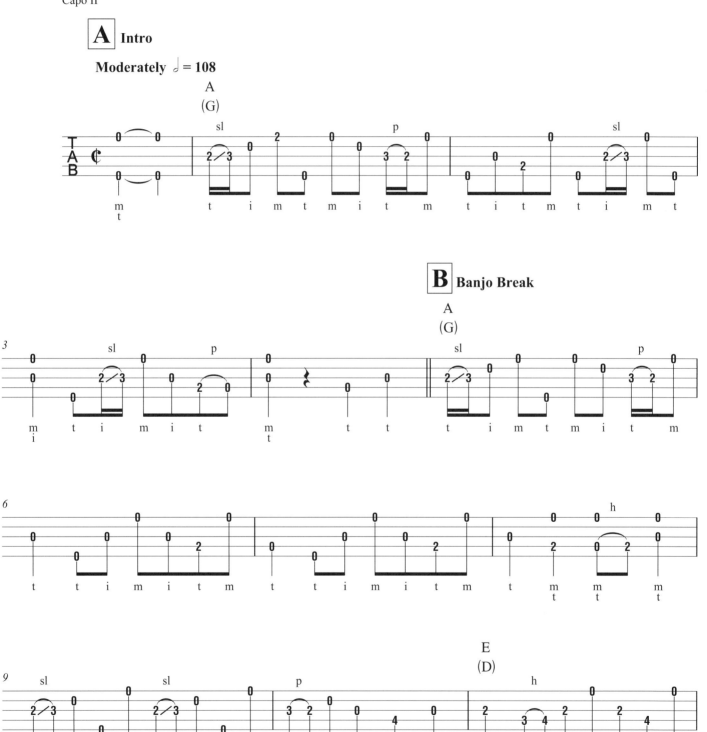

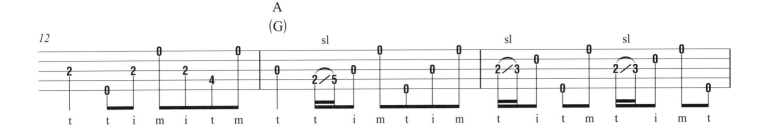

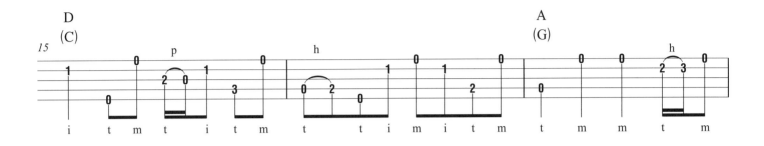

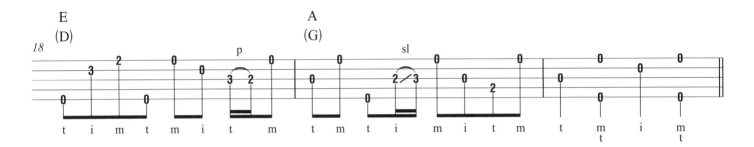

C Chorus

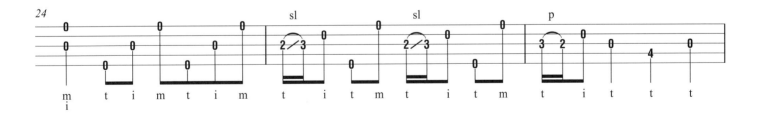

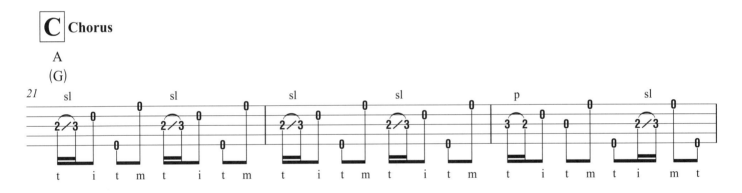

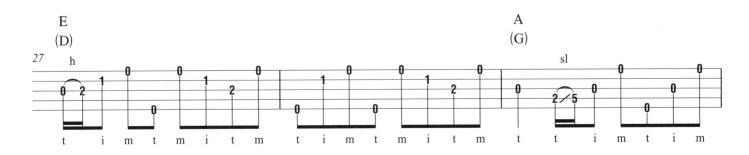

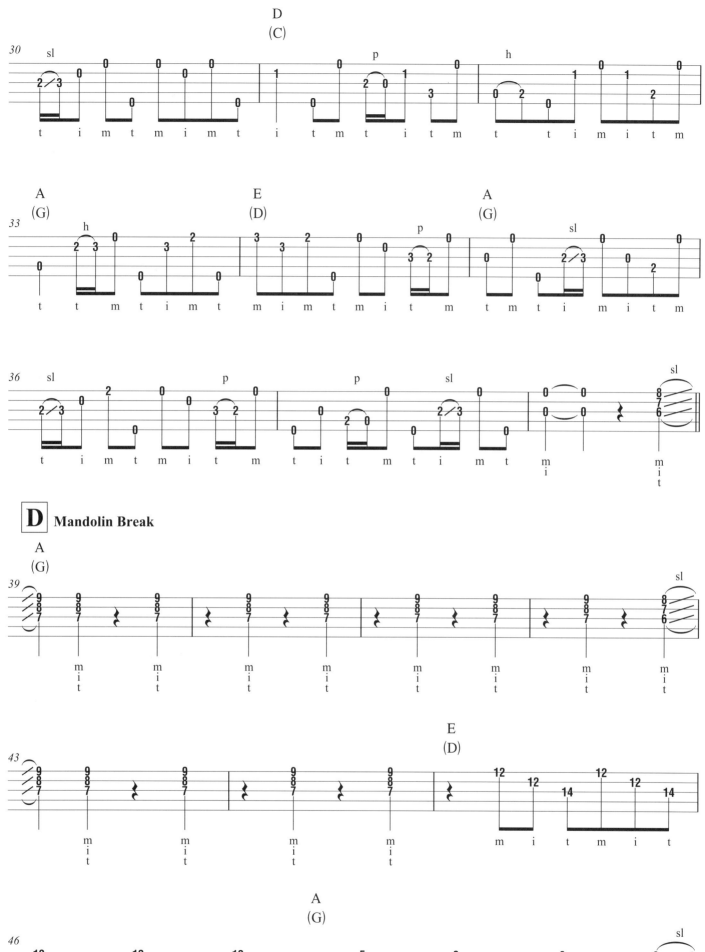

D Mandolin Break

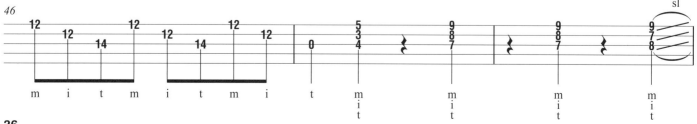

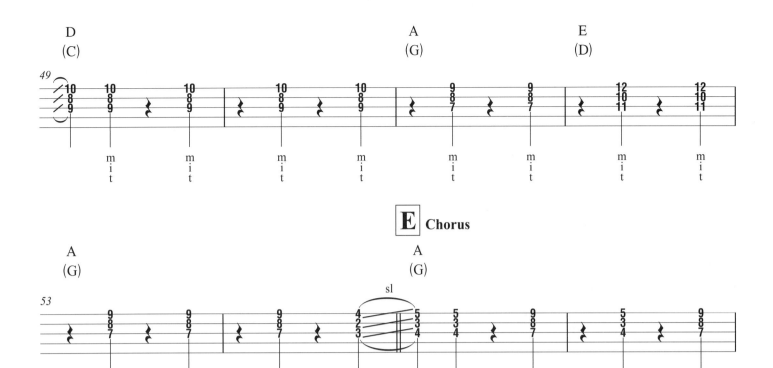

E Chorus

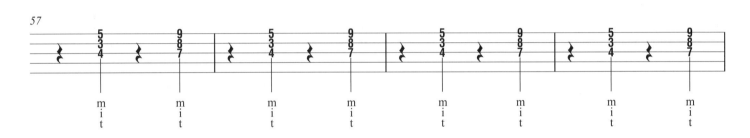

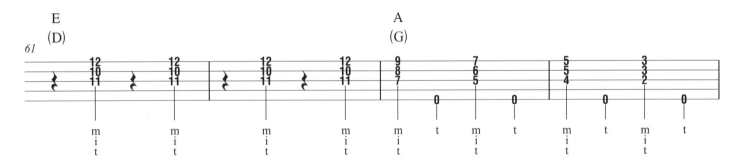

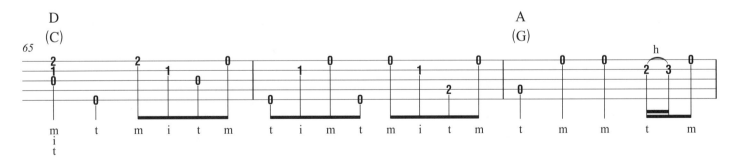

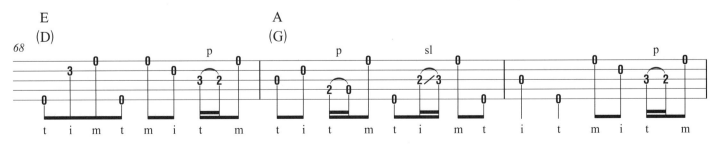

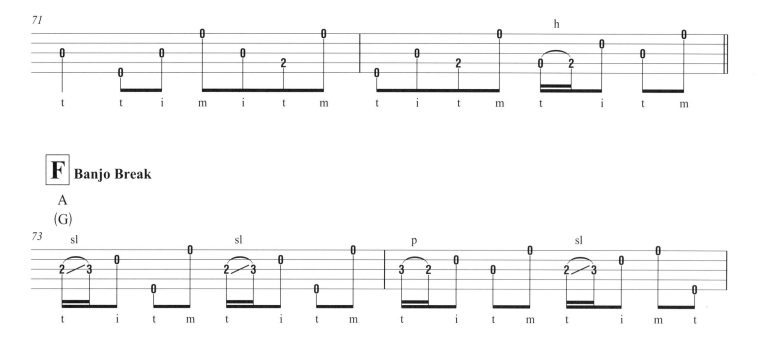

F Banjo Break

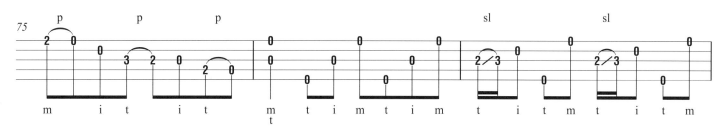

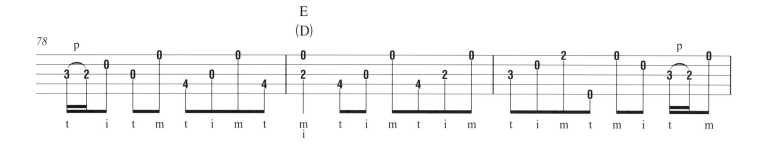

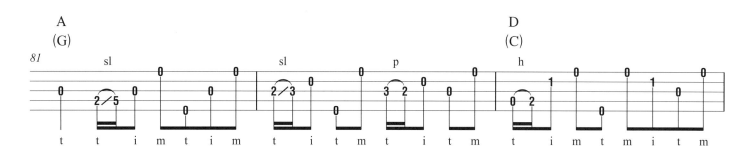

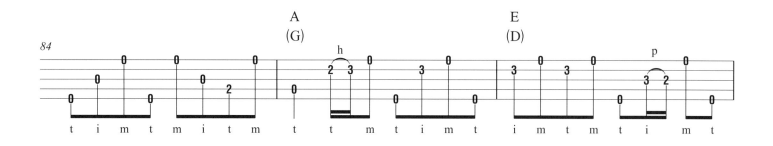

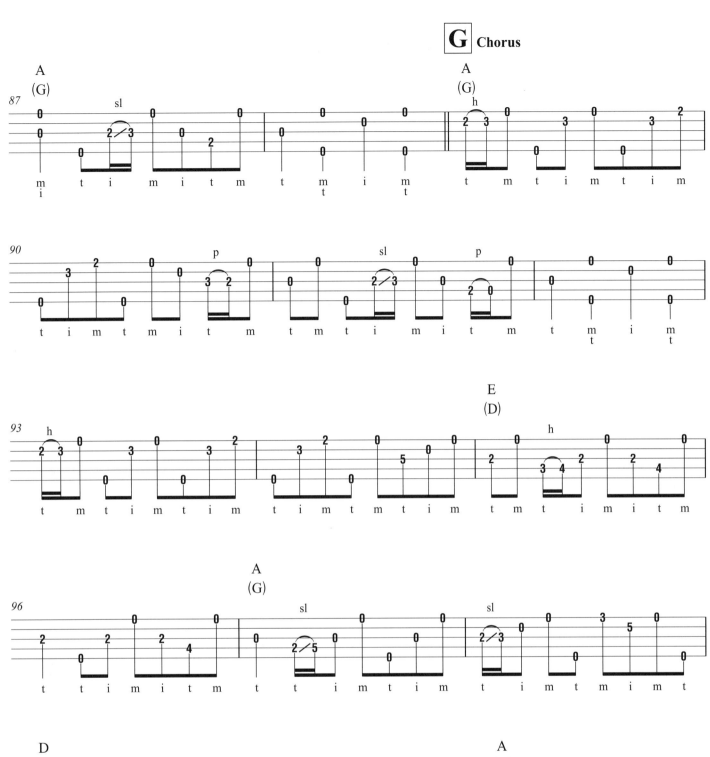

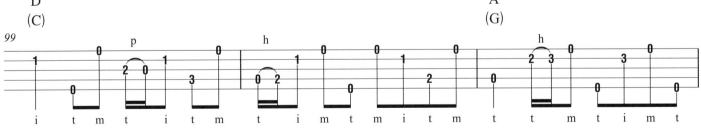

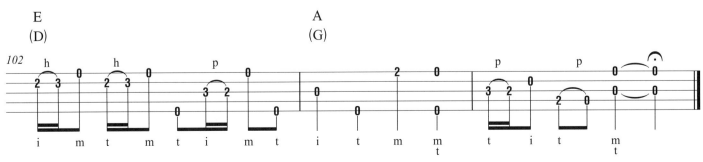

Wildwood Flower

Traditional

G tuning:
(5th-1st) G-D-G-B-D

Key of G

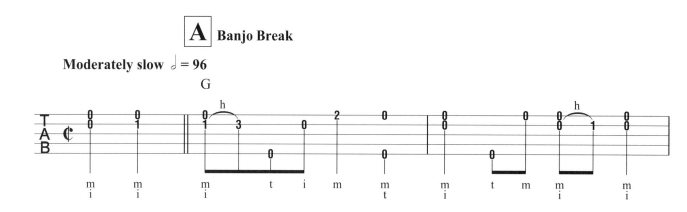

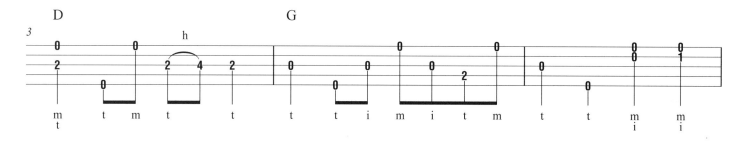

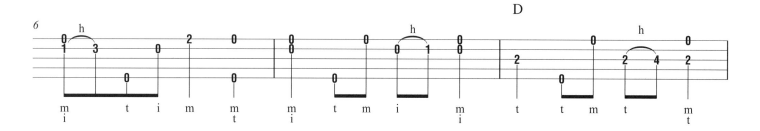

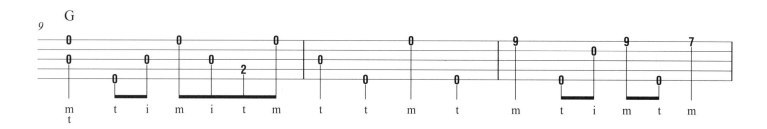

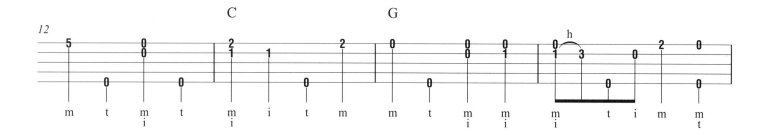

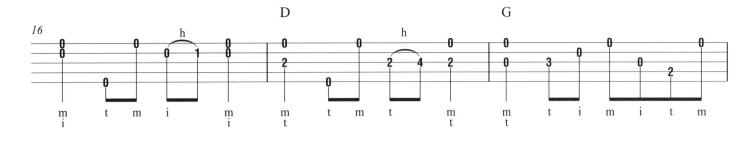

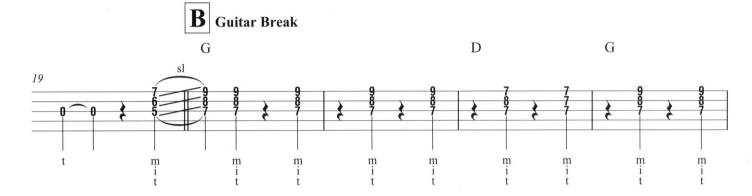

B Guitar Break

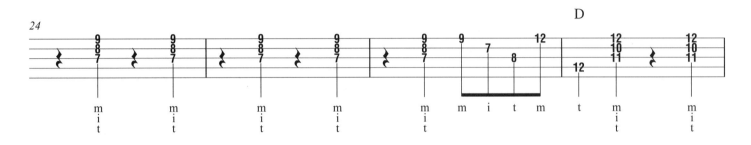

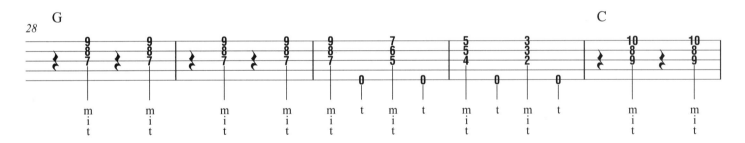

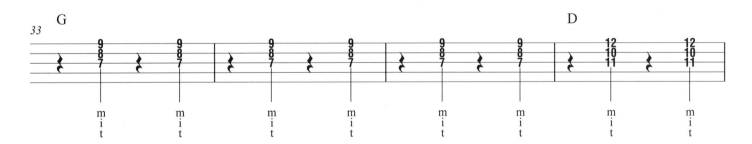

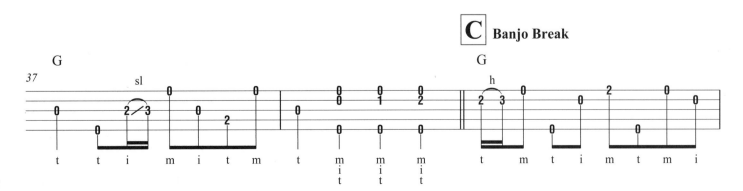

C Banjo Break

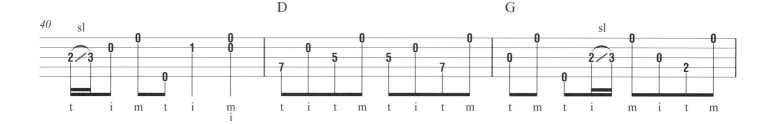

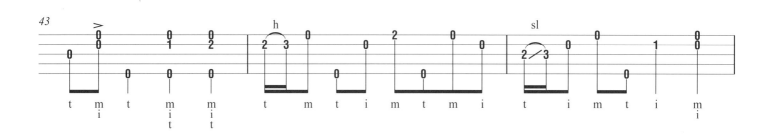

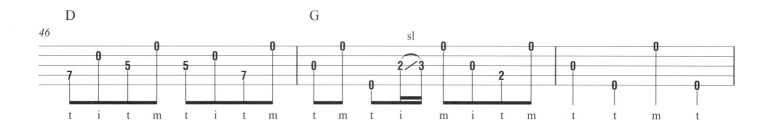

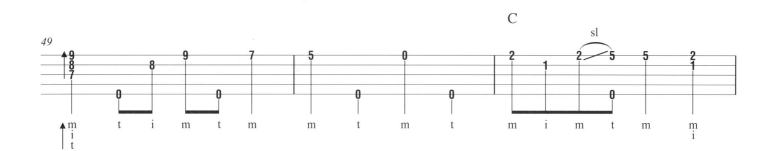

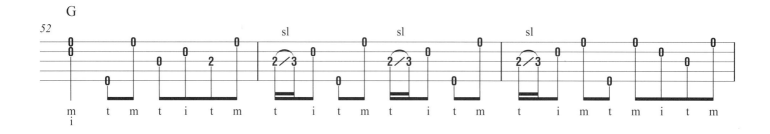

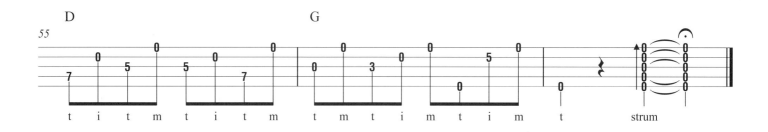

Endings
(Part A)

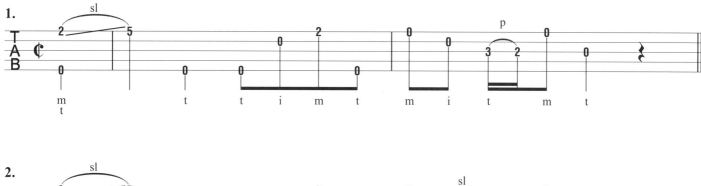

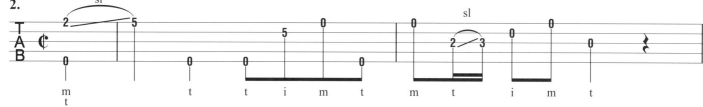

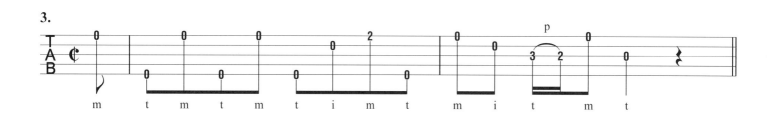

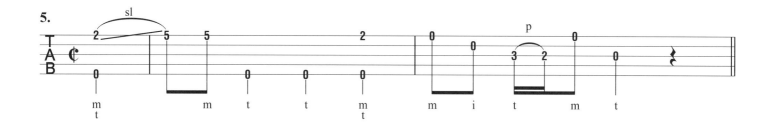

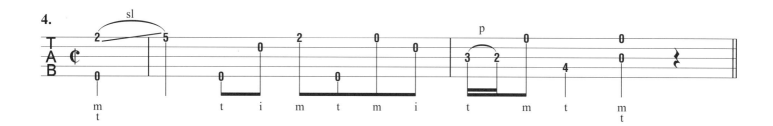

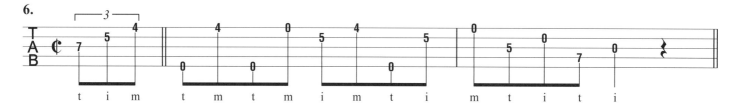

Endings
(Part B)

1.

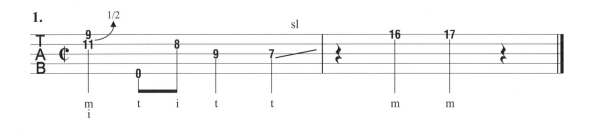

2.

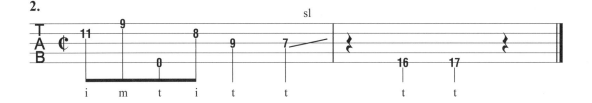

3.

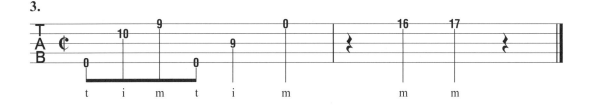

4.

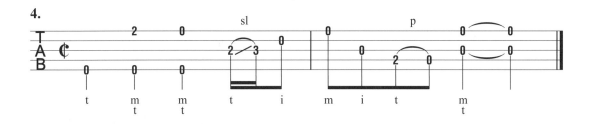

5.

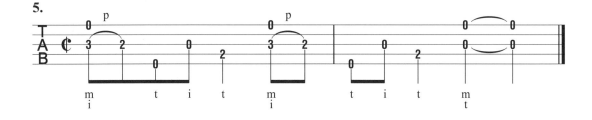

6.

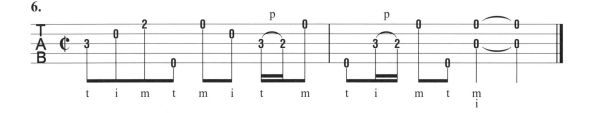

BANJO NOTATION LEGEND

TABLATURE graphically represents the banjo fingerboard. Each horizontal line represents a string, and each number represents a fret.

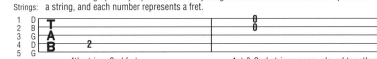

4th string, 2nd fret   1st & 2nd strings open, played together

TIME SIGNATURE:
The upper number indicates the number of beats per measure, the lower number indicates that a quarter note gets one beat.

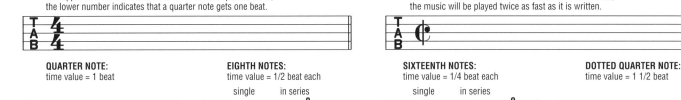

CUT TIME:
Each note's time value should be cut in half. As a result, the music will be played twice as fast as it is written.

QUARTER NOTE:
time value = 1 beat

EIGHTH NOTES:
time value = 1/2 beat each

single   in series

SIXTEENTH NOTES:
time value = 1/4 beat each

single   in series

DOTTED QUARTER NOTE:
time value = 1 1/2 beat

TIE: Pick the 1st note only, then let it sustain for the combined time value.

TRIPLET: Three notes played in the same time normally occupied by two notes of the same time value.

GRACE NOTE: A quickly played note with no time value of its own. The grace note and the note following it only occupy the time value of the second note.

RITARD: A gradual slowing of the tempo or speed of the song.

rit.

QUARTER REST:
time value = 1 beat of silence

EIGHTH REST:
time value = 1/2 beat of silence

HALF REST:
time value = 2 beats of silence

WHOLE REST:
time value = 4 beats of silence

ENDINGS: When a repeated section has a first and second ending, play the first ending only the first time and play the second ending only the second time.

1.   2.

REPEAT SIGNS: Play the music between the repeat signs two times.

D.S. AL CODA:
Play through the music until you complete the measure labeled *"D.S. al Coda,"* then go back to the sign (%).
Then play until you complete the measure labeled *"To Coda ⊕,"* then skip to the section labeled *"⊕ Coda."*

%   *To Coda* ⊕   *D.S. al Coda*   ⊕ *Coda*

HAMMER-ON: Strike the first (lower) note with one finger, then sound the higher note (on the same string) with another finger by fretting it without picking.

h
2 3

PULL-OFF: Place both fingers on the notes to be sounded. Strike the first note and without picking, pull the finger off to sound the second (lower) note.

p
3 2

SLIDE UP: Strike the first note and then slide the same fret-hand finger up to the second note. The second note is not struck.

s
2 5

SLIDE DOWN: Strike the first note and then slide the same fret-hand finger down to the second note. The second note is not struck.

s
4 2

HALF-STEP CHOKE: Strike the note and bend the string up 1/2 step.

1/2
7

WHOLE-STEP CHOKE: Strike the note and bend the string up one step.

1
10

NATURAL HARMONIC: Strike the note while the fret-hand lightly touches the string directly over the fret indicated.

Harm.
12

BRUSH: Play the notes of the chord indicated by quickly rolling them from bottom to top.

0
0
0
0

Scruggs/Keith Tuners:

HALF-TWIST UP: Strike the note, twist tuner up 1/2 step, and continue playing.

1/2
0

HALF-TWIST DOWN: Strike the note, twist tuner down 1/2 step, and continue playing.

1/2
0

WHOLE-TWIST UP: Strike the note, twist tuner up one step, and continue playing.

1
0

WHOLE-TWIST DOWN: Strike the note, twist tuner down one step, and continue playing.

1
0

Right Hand Fingerings
t = thumb   i = index finger   m = middle finger

Hal Leonard Banjo Play-Along Series

AUDIO ACCESS INCLUDED

The Banjo Play-Along Series will help you play your favorite songs quickly and easily with incredible backing tracks to help you sound like a bona fide pro! Just follow the banjo tab, listen to the demo track on the CD or online audio to hear how the banjo should sound, and then play along with the separate backing tracks. The CD is playable on any CD player and also is enhanced so Mac and PC users can adjust the recording to any tempo without changing the pitch! Books with online audio also include PLAYBACK+ options such as looping and tempo adjustments. Each Banjo Play-Along pack features eight cream of the crop songs.

INCLUDES TAB

1. BLUEGRASS
Ashland Breakdown • Deputy Dalton • Dixie Breakdown • Hickory Hollow • I Wish You Knew • I Wonder Where You Are Tonight • Love and Wealth • Salt Creek.
00102585 Book/CD Pack.........................$14.99

2. COUNTRY
East Bound and Down • Flowers on the Wall • Gentle on My Mind • Highway 40 Blues • If You've Got the Money (I've Got the Time) • Just Because • Take It Easy • You Are My Sunshine.
00105278 Book/CD Pack.........................$14.99

3. FOLK/ROCK HITS
Ain't It Enough • The Cave • Forget the Flowers • Ho Hey • Little Lion Man • Live and Die • Switzerland • Wagon Wheel.
00119867 Book/CD Pack.........................$14.99

4. OLD-TIME CHRISTMAS
Away in a Manger • Hark! the Herald Angels Sing • Jingle Bells • Joy to the World • O Holy Night • O Little Town of Bethlehem • Silent Night • We Wish You a Merry Christmas.
00119889 Book/CD Pack.........................$14.99

5. PETE SEEGER
Blue Skies • Get up and Go • If I Had a Hammer (The Hammer Song) • Kisses Sweeter Than Wine • Mbube (Wimoweh) • Sailing Down My Golden River • Turn! Turn! Turn! (To Everything There Is a Season) • We Shall Overcome.
00129699 Book/CD Pack.........................$17.99

6. SONGS FOR BEGINNERS
Bill Cheatham • Black Mountain Rag • Cripple Creek • Grandfather's Clock • John Hardy • Nine Pound Hammer • Old Joe Clark • Will the Circle Be Unbroken.
00139751 Book/CD Pack.........................$14.99

7. BLUEGRASS GOSPEL
Cryin' Holy unto the Lord • How Great Thou Art • I Saw the Light • I'll Fly Away • I'll Have a New Life • Man in the Middle • Turn Your Radio On • Wicked Path of Sin.
00147594 Book/Online Audio $14.99

8. CELTIC BLUEGRASS
Billy in the Low Ground • Cluck Old Hen • Devil's Dream • Fisher's Hornpipe • Little Maggie • Over the Waterfall • The Red Haired Boy • Soldier's Joy.
00160077 Book/Online Audio $14.99

Prices, contents, and availability subject to change without notice.

HAL•LEONARD®
www.halleonard.com

GREAT BANJO PUBLICATIONS

FROM HAL LEONARD

Hal Leonard Banjo Method – Second Edition

by Mac Robertson, Robbie Clement, Will Schmid

This innovative method teaches 5-string banjo bluegrass style using a carefully paced approach that keeps beginners playing great songs *while learning*. Book 1 covers easy chord strums, tablature, right-hand rolls, hammer-ons, slides and pull-offs, and more. Book 2 includes solos and licks, fiddle tunes, back-up, capo use, and more.

00699500	Book 1 Book Only	$7.99
00695101	Book 1 Book/Online Audio	$16.99
00699502	Book 2 Book Only	$7.99

Banjo Aerobics

A 50-Week Workout Program for Developing, Improving and Maintaining Banjo Technique

by Michael Bremer

Take your banjo playing to the next level with this fantastic daily resource, providing a year's worth of practice material with a two-week vacation. The accompanying audio includes demo tracks for all the examples in the book to reinforce how the banjo should sound.

00113734 Book/Online Audio $19.99

Banjo Chord Finder

This extensive reference guide covers over 2,800 banjo chords, including four of the most commonly used tunings. Thirty different chord qualities are covered for each key, and each chord quality is presented in two different voicings. Also includes a lesson on chord construction and a fingerboard chart of the banjo neck!

00695741 9 x 12.................... $6.99   00695742 6 x 9...................... $6.99

Banjo Scale Finder

by Chad Johnson

Learn to play scales on the banjo with this comprehensive yet easy-to-use book. It contains more than 1,300 scale diagrams for the most often-used scales and modes, including multiple patterns for each scale. Also includes a lesson on scale construction and a fingerboard chart of the banjo neck!

00695780 9 x 12.................... $9.99   00695783 6 x 9...................... $6.99

First 50 Songs You Should Play on Banjo

arr. Michael J. Miles & Greg Cahill

Easy-to-read banjo tab, chord symbols and lyrics for the most popular songs banjo players like to play. Explore clawhammer and three-finger-style banjo in a variety of tunings and capoings with this one-of-a-kind collection. Songs include: Angel from Montgomery • Carolina in My Mind • Cripple Creek • Danny Boy • The House of the Rising Sun • Mr. Tambourine Man • Take Me Home, Country Roads • This Land Is Your Land • Wildwood Flower • and many more.

00153311 ....$14.99

Fretboard Roadmaps

by Fred Sokolow

This handy book/with online audio will get you playing all over the banjo fretboard in any key! You'll learn to: increase your chord, scale and lick vocabulary • play chord-based licks, moveable major and blues scales, melodic scales and first-position major scales • and much more! The audio includes 51 demonstrations of the exercises.

00695358 Book/CD $15.99

O Brother, Where Art Thou?

Banjo tab arrangements of 12 bluegrass/folk songs from this Grammy-winning album. Includes: The Big Rock Candy Mountain • Down to the River to Pray • I Am a Man of Constant Sorrow • I Am Weary (Let Me Rest) • I'll Fly Away • In the Jailhouse Now • Keep on the Sunny Side • You Are My Sunshine • and more, plus lyrics and a banjo notation legend.

00699528 Banjo Tablature.. $14.99

Earl Scruggs and the 5-String Banjo

Earl Scruggs' legendary method has helped thousands of banjo players get their start. It features everything you need to know to start playing, even how to build your own banjo! Topics covered include: Scruggs tuners • how to read music • chords • how to read tablature • anatomy of Scruggs-style picking • exercises in picking • 44 songs • biographical notes • and more! The CD features Earl Scruggs playing and explaining over 60 examples!

00695764	Book Only	$22.99
00695765	Book/CD Pack	$34.99

Clawhammer Cookbook

Tools, Techniques & Recipes for Playing Clawhammer Banjo

by Michael Bremer

The goal of this book isn't to tell you how to play tunes or how to play like anyone else. It's to teach you ways to approach, arrange, and personalize any tune – to develop your own unique style. To that end, we'll take in a healthy serving of old-time music and also expand the clawhammer palate to taste a few other musical styles. Includes audio track demos of all the songs and examples to aid in the learning process.

00118354 Book/Online Audio.......................................$19.99

The Ultimate Banjo Songbook

A great collection of banjo classics: Alabama Jubilee • Bye Bye Love • Duelin' Banjos • The Entertainer • Foggy Mountain Breakdown • Great Balls of Fire • Lady of Spain • Orange Blossom Special • (Ghost) Riders in the Sky • Rocky Top • San Antonio Rose • Tennessee Waltz • UFO-TOFU • You Are My Sunshine • and more.

00699565 Book/Online Audio.................................... $27.50